T0104495

NEUCENTRIC BIBLICAL
WORKBOOKS

NEUCENTRIC BIBLICAL WORKBOOKS

Learning Gods Word
Genesis Chapter 1-10
Volume 1

Neu—Meaning New
Centric—Meaning Century

A New Century Way of Learning Exactly What God Says!

Rachel M. Sargent

authorHOUSE®

AuthorHouse™ LLC
1663 Liberty Drive
Bloomington, IN 47403
www.authorhouse.com
Phone: 1-800-839-8640

© 2014 Rachel M. Sargent. All rights reserved.

No part of this book may be reproduced, stored in a retrieval system, or transmitted
by any means without the written permission of the author.

Published by AuthorHouse   05/20/2014

ISBN: 978-1-4918-5034-3 (sc)
ISBN: 978-1-4918-5035-0 (e)

Library of Congress Control Number: 2014900507

Holy Bible, New International Version®, NIV® Copyright © 1973, 1978, 1984, 2011 by Biblica, Inc.®
Used by permission. All rights reserved worldwide.

Any people depicted in stock imagery provided by Thinkstock are models,
and such images are being used for illustrative purposes only.
Certain stock imagery © Thinkstock.

This book is printed on acid-free paper.

Because of the dynamic nature of the Internet, any web addresses or links contained in this book may have changed
since publication and may no longer be valid. The views expressed in this work are solely those of the author and do
not necessarily reflect the views of the publisher, and the publisher hereby disclaims any responsibility for them.

TABLE OF CONTENTS

INFORMATIONAL GUIDES:

Prayer is always my first and foremost guide

Various sermons from various pastors

Zondervan NIV Bible

Webster Dictionary

FOREWORDS

Malcolm Clyde Sargent—Brother

✠

First and foremost I would like to thank my Sister Rachel M. Sargent for introducing me to these incredible workbooks. I have worked intensively on the first three Neucentric Biblical Workbooks and they were very uplifting and enlightening to me emotionally and spiritually. These workbooks will not only help children, they will also help teenagers, young adults, and adults. These workbooks gave me a greater understanding to God's purposes for me, why He gave His only begotten son, the creation of Heaven and earth, and helped me to gain knowledge about the bible as well as an understanding of what God is saying in His word. These workbooks will help Christians of all ages grow and manifest in the Word of God.

Rachel, these workbooks were a fantastic idea

May God bless them and be with you in all you do.

Roosevelt Monroe Jr.—Son:

✠

Mom I want you to know that these workbooks help me a lot to understand how this world actually came to be and that there is a higher power I can go to. These workbooks are interesting and teach the Word of God in a new innovative way. I can honestly say I believe these workbooks will help people of all ages gain an interest in God's Word, have a relationship with Him, and pray to Him more.

Good job Mom!

Kianna Dajaunay Monroe—Daughter:

✠

I am thankful for my mom creating these workbooks for me so that I can keep reading the bible without being distracted or losing my train of thought because I could not understand what the bible was saying nor remember what I had read. Using these workbooks help me because I like to learn. Now I know exactly what God made on each day, that God forgives for sins if you repent, and that God helps and loves the poor and the fatherless, as well as, being able to remember what is written.

Thanks Mom you're the best!

Rachel M. Sargent

Riettamarie DeGraffe—Sister in Christ

✝

When reading or studying the Bible we often bypass small details in search of specifics we may be looking for. While assisting with the task of proofreading this workbook I have discovered some details that I might not otherwise have seen. The idea of these types of workbooks as a study aid is of tremendous value. I have gained a deeper level of appreciation for the specifics found in the Word of God. This is a great undertaking and I am honored to be a part of it.

PREFACE

Neucentric Biblical workbooks are a series of questions from Genesis to Revelations that comes directly from the Zondervan NIV Study Bible. These workbooks are formatted as a series of volumes for each book of the bible. These workbooks are a new century way for all ages to learn Gods' word exactly how it is written in efforts to help those with a zeal for God's word gain knowledge of God's word that all may lead a structured and prosperous life by having a relationship with our Lord and Savior Jesus Christ. *{Hosea 4:6 NIV} states: My people are destroyed through lack of knowledge. "Because you have rejected knowledge, I also reject you as my priest; because you have ignored the law of your God, I also will ignore your children."*

Many parents fail to be able to help their children from the ways of the world and bring up their children in the way they should go because they themselves lack the knowledge of the Word and the commands of God. *{John 1:1 NIV} states: in the beginning was the Word, and the Word was with God, and the Word was God.*

These workbooks have been viewed and enjoyed by people ages 9-47 its content consist of various learning exercises such as:

- *Spelling Words—an exercise that helps the reader to learn how to spell various words, mentioned various times, throughout the bible.*

- *ABC order: an exercise that is a fun way to enhance the reader's ability to put things in order and become familiar with alphabetizing.*

- *Unscrambling word: an exercise that helps to train the reader's thoughts to look into the Word for the answers.*

- *Fill in the blank: an exercise that will help the reader to remember what he/she is reading by writing the missing word and pointing out certain key words in the chapter.*

- *Simplified Questions: an exercise that helps the reader understand and say exactly what the Scripture say without adding or taking away from the Scripture.*

- *Essays: an exercise that helps the reader to put each biblical passage in a modern day example as a final authority for them to deal with life's daily challenges in a godly manner.*

- *Unit reviews: an exercise that helps the reader to exercise the revelations God has given to him/her that they may gain an understanding through the fullness of His word.*

- *Map Study exercises (Not all workbooks will have this feature.): These exercises will help the reader visualize biblical journey, the area, what was happening, and why it took God to lead Israel through their Journey to give thought as to why we also need God to guide us through our trials and tribulations.*

- *Answer key for all exercises and questions are in the back of the book.*

(To get direct answers to all questions and definitions in this workbook, the Zondervan NIV study bible and the Webster dictionary must be used.)

ACKNOWLEDGEMENTS

I acknowledge, first and foremost, giving honor and glory to my heavenly Father. Father I thank you for sending my Lord and Savior Jesus Christ as a sacrificial atonement for my sins, my freedom, my redemption, and my salvation.

I thank, praise, and worship my Lord and Savior Jesus Christ for His divine mercy that has allowed me to enter into His grace. Even though, my righteousness are as filthy rags in His sight and I continue to fall short of the glory You still show Your mercy upon me. Thank You Lord and Savior for bringing me out of darkness and into Your glorious light.

I thank you Lord and Savior for sending the power of the Holy Spirit to comfort me and help me to learn Your Word that I may receive the revelations to the secrets keys to the Kingdom, live a life worthy of my calling, while being guided, protected and given soundness of mind.

I thank the power of the Holy Spirit for divine covering, shielding, guiding, and filling my soul with the power of prayer, praise, and worship unto my Lord and Savior Jesus Christ.

I thank the Holy Spirit for teaching and guiding me through each chapter and each verse of the bible from start to finish of these workbooks.

I say thank You to the Father, thank You to the Son, and thank You to the Holy Spirit for this wonderful gift of written ministry and for using me to help edify the body of Christ.

Thank You for each pastor You have placed my footsteps in the path of, (my feet move according to Your will), to preach Your word as they are the voices that made these workbooks possible.

I give a special thank you to all the pastors that God have placed in my life to help me to grow into this new being in Christ. Each Pastor helped to nurture the different gifts the Lord has given to me and my zeal to know God. In the order in which God has allowed our paths to join together in unity for His will and purposes: Pastor Marvin D. Hooks; Reverend Lisa Maye; Reverend Cheryl Walker; Pastor A. G. Chancellor; and Pastor Anthony Seaton.

Pastor Anthony Seaton & his wife 1ˢᵗ Lady Barbara Seaton

✢

I would like to give special thanks to Pastor Anthony and first lady Barbara Seaton who have been tremendous spiritual leaders. I look to them as brilliant spiritual parents whose leadership have help to put great revelation into me that I may in turn release this information into these workbooks. Also, I thank the both of them for welcoming me into their body of Christ with open arms and an unexplainable love that gives one a greater understanding to the meaning of being connected to the body of Christ in unity through love, word, with the application of His love and word together to form unity in the body of Christ. Pastor I would also like to thank you for allowing me to utilize the many revelations you have given me, throughout many of your teachings, into these workbooks as much of the New Testament revelation has come from your guidance in the Word.

Pastor Marvin Dewitt Hooks

✢

Pastor Hooks I thank God for allowing our paths to meet. I thank you for going over the first workbook for me and for your idea to include ABC-order and Definitions in an answer key page to help make it easier on the children when they begin to learn from these workbooks. Through your ministry I have learned how to be patient and wait on God and, how to be sure of my calling. I would also like to thank you for your many prayers, your patience, and time you have taken to help me with the many questions I have had concerning Scripture. Much of my theological aspect in the book of Genesis came from the sermons you preached and the questions you have taken time to answer for me. Pastor thank you and may God continue to bless you, your family, and the St. Mary A.M.E Zion church family that you remain an awesome blessing to our communities.

Reverend Lisa Maye

✢

Reverend Maye I never thought I would walk into a church of any kind and walking into St. Mary's A.M.E. Zion church I was nervous, somewhat confused, and felt out of place. As I sat there in the back pew listening to your sermon I felt as though the Lord was speaking to me through his woman of God. Going through most of my life feeling out of place as if I didn't belong; the words that came from your mouth in that sermon made me feel I was finally in the right place and kept me returning to that place. I want to thank you and let you know that these workbooks may not have come about if you weren't there to give that sermon on that Sunday evening. May God continue to bless and use you in the lives of many that that they may (as I have) release each seed planted in them by you and the saints at St. Mary's A.M.E. Zion Church.

Reverend Cheryl Walker

☦

Reverend Cheryl I would like to thank you for your many prayers that have helped me to elevate in my walk in Christ. Your encouraging sermons has given me the ability to rise against all odds knowing this battle is not my own but it is the Lords. Reverend Cheryl it was a pleasure working with you at the outreach at St. Mary's A.M.E. Zion church. I have gained much knowledge by your examples of kindness, your boldness in Christ, and your ability to deliver a powerful message that one can readily apply to their life. Thank you Reverend Cheryl and may God continue to be with you and the St. Mary A.M.E. Zion church family guiding and instructing you in the good works of our communities.

Pastor A.G. Chancellor III & his wife 1st Lady Barbara Chancellor

☦

Pastor Chancellor I thank you for the devoted bible studies you give every Wednesday night at Mount Olive Baptist Church. It was through these bible studies that I learned how to actually read the word of God and focus on gaining an understanding, while researching the text in its entirety. God's blessing for me to attend your bible study services enhanced the writing abilities given unto me, from the Lord, for the purpose of beginning this written ministry as a gift to the body of Christ at large. Your powerful preaching and teaching ministry has helped me tremendously. You teach us to study the fullness of the text as it is written, write in essay form what we have received from the message, and to look beyond what we see written in our carnal minds, seek the spiritual revelation in how we can focus that Scripture into our lives. It is my belief that the Lord sent me to your ministry for you to bring forth this gift of teaching He has placed in me and the ability to use the gift of written ministry He has given me as a measure to format what is written in His Holy Word into workbook form. It is my belief that by the wonderful outcome of these workbooks; you have done an awesome job helping me to understand the word enough to break each verse down and format a series of questions and answer that all can come to gain an understanding of the Word of God.

Reverend Dr. Beresford Adams

☦

Reverend Dr. Beresford Adams I would like to give you a special thank you for your guidance in my walk with Jesus. I haven't had the privilege to be a part of your church ministry; however, God has allowed me to be a part of your communicable services that you have provided in many communities. Having served as a part of the NAACP with you and Sister Phyllis Butler helped my growth in many ways. Watching your meek humble character gave me the faith I needed to continue on in my walk with Christ as well as this good work the Lord has put in me with these workbooks. I thank you and I thank God for allowing me the privilege to have my footsteps meet the same paths of His man of God. May God continue to bless you, your family, and the Faith Baptist church family and continue use you in such a divine way blessing the hands of your work into divine prosperity.

Elder Angela Ramdoo

✠

Elder Ramdoo I would like to thank you for your nurturing in the Word of God, for the fellowship you have taken time out of your busy weekly schedule to hold in your home, and helping me to mature in Christ. I have greatly benefited from your gift of ministering and thank you for taking out the time to answer many questions I have had concerning the Holy Scriptures. I would like you to know your phone conversations, your open home, and open arms have given me more than what was needed to finish this good work put in me by God. Elder Ramdoo you have given me foundation by example to stand on the Word of God and I thank you for all your encouragement, your prayers, and your rebuke of the adversary making sure I understood God has the final authority over my life.

Sister Jacquiline McClary

✠

I would like to give thanks to a wonderful sister in Christ, Mrs. McClary you have taken me on as a student and nurtured great abilities within me that I was afraid to face, as well as, making it possible for me to verbally communicate my visions from the Lord. Watching your organizational skills as you have taught them to me during my volunteering at the church/school has given me great preparation to carry into my personal and spiritual life.

Sister Riettamarie DeGraffe

✠

Sister Rietta I would like to thank you for taking the time out of your busy schedule to proofread this workbook. Your encouragement helped me to continue to go on with these workbooks that all can receive a greater understand of the Holy Scriptures and the revelations in which the Lord reveals unto to them. Thank you for making me smile when I want to cry; hold on when I want to let go; and understand situations when I want to attack them.

Sister Diane Wilson

✠

Sister Diane, thank you for your encouragement and planting the seed of hope in me that the mustard seed of faith already in me activated. The divine uplifting and encouragement that you gave to me was in such great abundance that until this day I do not have the words to describe. It is sisters in Christ like you; that help those coming to Christ know though they may feel out of place; they are in the right place and Christians like you are how they know God has called them into and not them running to! Your open home, arms, and advice is and will always be greatly appreciated. To me you are a one and a million. My dear sister in Christ may God continue to bless you that you may give all He sends in your path this same seed of hope to carry on in their walk with Jesus.

Sister Phyllis Butler

✛

Sister Phyllis you are a woman of noble character and I thank you for your guidance and patience. The affect you made on, not only me but my daughter also, I am grateful unto the Lord for allowing our paths to meet. As I watched your patience while you taught my daughter it helped my teaching abilities to grow in patience, understanding, and humbleness. Your dedication to the children in the community gave me a greater understanding to the meaning of devotion. Thank you for the kindness you have bestowed upon me and my daughter. These are memories that shall last a lifetime; encouragements that shall continue to help us grow; and confirmation that we can do all things through Christ who strengthens us.

Lavern Hayes

✛

Lavern I would thank you for all your much appreciated help. When I thought I wouldn't make it another day; you were there, When I needed someone just to listen to my cry; you were there, when I needed a place to continue to work on these workbooks; you were there, you have been such an encouragement and a role model for me to not give up on myself. I dedicate these workbooks to you as you were the nurturing force from the start of them. Thank you my dear friend when I needed one and Duwane Jackson thank you for sharing your mom with me.

My Family &Friends
Alexander William Sargent
(My Granddaddy)

✛

Granddaddy Alex, your love, embrace, and uplifting encouraging words have brought me through so much in my life. Having so much of you in me keeps you alive through me. Memories of you give me an inner strength too powerful to describe. I dedicate these workbooks to you as just a small token of my appreciation unto you. Granddaddy Alex you have always taught me to fly high; grab all that I can imagine and make it a reality; build on solid ground and not wavering waters or shaky ground and I would know the difference between the three by how it grows. I now build on the Solid Rock (Jesus).

William Alexander & Delphine Loveday-Sargent
(Dad) & (Mom)

✝

Dad my love for you will never cease; memories increase day to day. When I feel down I just remember the day I asked you are dreams real and do dreams come true; you held me in your arms and said: "Well sister Rae-Rae; that would be up to you! I then asked do you dream; your reply was: "I have a dream that one day one of my children will enter into college and get a business degree; I believe that child is going to be you!" Dad I cherish the many memories of you instilling just how much I can be and how far I would; doing this gave me the mindset to reach far beyond what anyone said or thought I would not be. You have left us, but oh, how I wish your eyes were here to see this God given blessing from the Trinity. I love you dad your discipline and wisdom did not go in one ear or out the other; it, nurtured me within healing my pain and keeping me sane not one sacrifice you've made has been in vain.

I would like to thank my children: my daughter Delphine Rene Sargent, my son Jacob James Shaw Jr., my son Roosevelt Monroe Jr., my daughter Salan Dee Monroe, and my daughter Kianna Dajaunay Monroe for all the time they have allowed me to take from them and put into these workbooks. Your willingness to sacrifice mom for the glory of God is appreciated. Jacob I thank you for your help in the financial process of these workbooks and Kianna I thank you for bringing this idea forward unto me and believing in your mom to fulfill the thoughts you have brought forward to her.

I would like to thank all my siblings: my brother John G. Sargent, Sister Belinda D. Sargent, Brother Malcolm C. Sargent, William A. Sargent Jr., Debra R. Sargent, Yolanda D. Sargent, Sonni G. Sargent, and Lawrence A. Sargent for all their encouragement over the years. Each of you have helped me to grow and achieve all that I could imagine throughout my life. Debra I thank you for making your home available to me that the process of these workbooks continued without ceasing. Malcolm I thank you for being there with uplift words at times I wanted to give up. William I thank you for your encouraging words, your protection, your guidance, and always being there. I also thank you for helping in the financial process of these workbooks and the many good things you have helped me to accomplish throughout my life.

I would like to give special tribute to all my nieces and nephews who have helped me to maintain with their encouraging words and just simply being a part of my life. I hope that these workbooks can help you to move forward in the Lord: Janelle Sargent-Serrano, Shatavia Sargent-White, Alexandria Sargent, John Sargent Jr., Shaquawna Chinn, Amena Chinn, Latisha Sargent, William Sargent III, Gregory Sargent, Deirdre Sargent, Tanisha Sargent, Victoria Simmons, Shanika Simmons, Dashaun Simmons, Jermaine Austin, Jerome Austin.

I would like to give a special thank you to all of my grandchildren whom I pray I will personally teach from these workbooks and help their relationship with Jesus Christ elevate as they grow: Tionce' L. K. Laird, Amaya M. Monroe, Kahliyah A. Dunn, Jada A. Shaw, Roosevelt M. A. Monroe III, Javion J. Shaw, and Kahmaya A. Dunn may God be with you and keep His hedge of protection around you and guide you unto His word and will for each of your lives.

Before getting started let's get to know our bibles.

The Old Testament has 39 books:

1. Genesis	14. 2nd Chronicles	27. Daniel
2. Exodus	15. Ezra	28. Hosea
3. Leviticus	16. Nehemiah	29. Joel
4. Numbers	17. Esther	30. Amos
5. Deuteronomy	18. Job	31. Obadiah
6. Joshua	19. Psalms	32. Jonah
7. Judges	20. Proverbs	33. Micah
8. Ruth	21. Ecclesiastes	34. Nahum
9. 1st Samuel	22. Song of Songs	35. Habakkuk
10. 2nd Samuel	23. Isaiah	36. Zephaniah
11. 1st Kings	24. Jeremiah	37. Haggai
12. 2nd Kings	25. Lamentations	38. Zechariah
13. 1st Chronicles	26. Ezekiel	39. Malachi

There are five books of Pentateuch/Law:

1. Genesis

2. Exodus

3. Leviticus

4. Numbers

5. Deuteronomy

The first five books of the Bible are the books of Law recorded to inform all about the beginning of creation, God's commandments, covenants, promises, blessings, and deliverance for those of righteousness, as well as, God's destruction for man's disobedience. As Adam's disobedience brought about death to all who follow the wiles of the devil, Noah's belief and obedience brought about covenants to all generations; Abraham's faith brought about blessings and promises to all nations, which lead to the coming of our Lord and Savior Jesus Christ whose obedience to be a sacrificial atonement for the sins of all the nations brought Salvation, Redemption, Freedom, and the dispensation of Mercy and Grace.

There are twelve books of History:

1. Joshua

2. Judges

3. Ruth

4. 1st Samuel

5. 2nd Samuel

6. 1st Kings

> The next twelve books are the books of history recorded to give encouragement and assurance of God's rewards for the obedience of the people; to illustrate the importance and value of godliness, obedience, loyalty, and faithfulness among the nations; warnings of destruction as well as, the consequences for disobeying God and His commandments; and to illustrate that God is a God of restoration and deliverance to all who obey His commandments and walk in obedience, godliness, loyalty, and faithfulness unto Him; as well as, a God of destruction to all who turn from Him and disobey His commands and ordinances.

7. 2nd Kings

8. 1st Chronicles

9. 2nd Chronicles

10. Ezra

11. Nehemiah

12. Esther

There are twelve books of Prophecy. The first five books of prophecy are the books of Major Prophets:

1. Isaiah

2. Jeremiah

3. Lamentation

4. Ezekiel

5. Daniel

> The next five books are the books of prophecy recorded to warn Israel of the judgments that were to come, have come, and is still to come, visions of the prophets, illustrates the loss of Israel's land, city, and temple because of disobedience, the importance of repentance and hope. These prophetic revelations have been prophetically revealed to the apostle John in the book of Revelation to warn all of what is to come. These books reveal the coming of our Messiah in Isaiah 9:6 "This child born unto us has brought Salvation, Redemption, and Freedom of sins through repentance for all nations who follow the commands/ Laws of God."

The next twelve books of prophecy are the books of the Minor Prophets:

1. Hosea

2. Joel

3. Amos

4. Obadiah

5. Jonah

6. Micah

7. Nahum

8. Habakkuk

9. Zephaniah

10. Haggai

11. Zechariah

12. Malachi

> *The next twelve books are the books of the minor prophets recorded to warn all of the adulteries of Judah and Israel; call all to repentance of sins; help us to understand that God loves all, to give hope to all; to bring forth self-examination as God examines the hearts and mind of mankind; to help us to understand the value of God's mercy. As written in Jonah 4:2 God gives warning before destruction that you may repent and be saved.*

There are five books of Poetry:

1. Job

2. Psalms

3. Proverbs

4. Ecclesiastes

5. Song of Songs
    Or Song of Solomon

> *The next five books are the books of poetry/wisdom recorded to illustrate the sovereignty of God's faithfulness even in times of our trials and tribulations. These books of poetry/wisdom help us to understand God's guidance, blessings, and provision for all who endure to the end. These books include the God-given wisdom, hymns, proverbs, and worship of Israel while demonstrating the importance of prayer, praise, and worship unto God as it is our prayer, praise, and worship unto God which activates the manifestation of our blessings through communication with our Lord and Savior.*

> ** Note the books of Psalm are not categorized as chapter and verses like all the other books of the Bible. The Books of Psalms are classified as five books and one hundred-fifty divisions:*
>
> *Book 1: Divisions 1-41*
> *Book 2: Divisions 42-72*
> *Book 3: Divisions 73-89*
> *Book 4: Divisions 90-106*
> *Book 5: Divisions 107-150*

The Beginning

Spelling/Definition words write each word 3xs each:

Created			
Hovering			
Separated			
Produce			
Livestock			
Image			
Expanse			
Teem			
Surface			
Formless			

Write each word in ABC order:

Created	
Hovering	
Separated	
Produce	
Livestock	
Image	
Expanse	
Teem	
Surface	
Formless	

Using your spelling words—unscramble each word below:

CUREFAS	
NAXSEPE	
METE	
GIMAE	
RHINEVOG	
SLEMSOFR	
DATEPASE	
DARETEC	
CODEDUP	
COVESLITK	

Write the definition for each word:

1. Created:

   _____
   _____
   _____
   _____
   _____
   _____

2. Hovering:

   _____
   _____
   _____
   _____
   _____
   _____

3. Separate:

   _____
   _____
   _____
   _____
   _____
   _____

4. Produce:

   _____
   _____
   _____
   _____
   _____
   _____

5. Livestock:

   _____
   _____
   _____
   _____
   _____
   _____

6. Image:

7. Expanse:

8. Teem:

9. Surface:

10. Formless:

Genesis Chapter 1

The Beginning

1. What did God create in the beginning?

   _____
   _____
   _____
   _____

2. What was hovering over the waters?

   _____
   _____
   _____
   _____

3. What did God say concerning light?

   _____
   _____
   _____
   _____

4. What did God do with the light?

   _____
   _____
   _____
   _____

5. What did God call light and darkness?

   _____
   _____
   _____
   _____

6. What did God say concerning the waters?

   _____
   _____
   _____
   _____

7. What did God do with the expanse He created?

   _____
   _____
   _____
   _____

8. What did God call the expanse?

_____
_____
_____
_____

9. What was created on the second day?

_____
_____
_____
_____

10. What did God gather to one place and what appeared when He did this?

_____
_____
_____
_____

11. What did God call the dry ground and waters and what did He see about them?

_____
_____
_____
_____

12. What did God say concerning the production of the land?

_____
_____
_____
_____

13. What did the land then produce?

_____
_____
_____
_____

14. What was there on the third day and what did God see about it?

_____
_____
_____
_____

15. What did God say concerning the light?

_____
_____
_____
_____

16. How many lights did God make and what did He create them to do?

_____

_____

_____

_____

17. Why did God also make the stars?

_____

_____

_____

_____

18. What was on the fourth day?

_____

_____

_____

_____

19. What did God say let the waters and birds do?

_____

_____

_____

_____

20. How does the text describe God's creation of creatures and what did God see about His creation?

_____

_____

_____

_____

21. What did God say to bless His creation?

_____

_____

_____

_____

22. What was created on the fifth day?

_____

_____

_____

_____

23. What did God say to let the land produce?

_____

_____

_____

_____

24. Why does God say "Let's make man?"

_____

_____

_____

_____

25. How did God create man?

_____

_____

_____

_____

26. What did God say to bless man?

_____

_____

_____

_____

27. What had God given to man?

_____

_____

_____

_____

28. What did God see about all He created?

_____

_____

_____

_____

29. What was on the sixth day?

_____

_____

_____

_____

Written Essay#1

God saw all He made was good. Write a brief essay explaining how you should also see all that you do in your daily production is good before you say "it is so."

_____
_____
_____
_____
_____
_____
_____
_____
_____
_____
_____
_____
_____
_____
_____
_____
_____
_____
_____
_____
_____
_____
_____
_____
_____
_____
_____
_____
_____
_____
_____
_____
_____
_____
_____
_____
_____
_____

Written Essay #2

On each day God created something, with the exception of the seventh day. Write a brief essay on how you can follow God from day to day in being productive on each day and is there an importance for us to also rest on the seventh day and why:

_____
_____
_____
_____
_____
_____
_____
_____
_____
_____
_____
_____
_____
_____
_____
_____
_____
_____
_____
_____
_____
_____
_____
_____
_____
_____
_____
_____
_____
_____
_____
_____
_____
_____

Adam and Eve

Spelling/Definition Words write each word 3xs each:

Suitable			
Command			
Good			
United			
Shame			
Seed			
Vast			
Array			
Account			
Evil			

Write each word in ABC order:

Suitable	
Command	
Good	
United	
Shame	
Seed	
Vast	
Array	
Account	
Evil	

Using your spelling words—unscramble each word below:

TVAS	
MEHAS	
LIVE	
RAYAR	
DOGO	
CUTNOCA	
BLUETASI	
TUNEDI	
DESE	
DOMCANM	

Write the definition for each word:

1. Suitable:

2. Command:

3. Good:

4. United:

5. Shame:

6. Seed:

7. Vast:

8. Array:

9. Account:

10. Evil:

Genesis Chapter 2

The Beginning (cont.)/Adam and Eve

The Beginning (cont.)

1. What did the Lord God state was complete?

    _____

    _____

    _____

    _____

2. When did God finish the work he had been doing and rest?

    _____

    _____

    _____

    _____

3. Why did God bless the seventh day?

    _____

    _____

    _____

    _____

Adam and Eve

4. What account does the inspired writer give us in the book of Genesis?

    _____

    _____

    _____

    _____

5. How does the inspired writer describe how God made the heavens and the earth?

    _____

    _____

    _____

    _____

6. Where did the Lord God plant a garden?

    _____

    _____

    _____

    _____

7. Where did the Lord God put the man he had formed?

_____

_____

_____

_____

8. What did the Lord make grow out of the ground, how was this to his sight, and what were they good for?

_____

_____

_____

_____

9. What was in the middle of the garden?

_____

_____

_____

_____

10. What flowed from Eden and what did it separate to?

_____

_____

_____

_____

11. What was the name of the first water-head and how is it described?

_____

_____

_____

_____

12. What was in that land and what was called good there?

_____

_____

_____

_____

13. What was the name of the second water-head and where did it wind through?

_____

_____

_____

_____

14. What was the name of the third water-head and what did it run along?

_____

_____

_____

_____

15. What was the name of the fourth water-head?

_____

_____

_____

_____

16. Why did the Lord take man and place him in the Garden of Eden?

_____

_____

_____

_____

17. What command did the Lord God give man?

_____

_____

_____

_____

18. What did the Lord God say concerning man being alone?

_____

_____

_____

_____

19. What did the Lord God form out of the ground?

_____

_____

_____

_____

20. What was not found for Adam and what did the Lord God do as a result?

_____

_____

_____

_____

21. How did the Lord God make woman and where did He bring her?

_____

_____

_____

_____

22. What did Adam say when God brought the woman to him?

_____
_____
_____
_____

23. What did God say man should do for this reason?

_____
_____
_____
_____

24. Were the man and his wife clothed or naked and were they ashamed or not ashamed?

_____
_____
_____
_____

Written Essay

Write a brief essay explaining how this chapter can help you to understand how God feel about you and the things He knows you are missing without you having to ask Him:

_____
_____
_____
_____
_____
_____
_____
_____
_____
_____
_____
_____
_____
_____
_____
_____
_____
_____
_____

GENESIS CHAPTER 3
The fall of Man

Spelling/Definition words write each word 3xs each:

Crafty			
Serpent			
Enmity			
Thorns			
Guard			
Thistles			
Banish			
Desire			
Cursed			
Garment			

Write each word in ABC order:

Crafty	
Serpent	
Enmity	
Thorns	
Guard	
Thistles	
Banish	
Desire	
Cursed	
Garment	

Using your spelling words—unscramble each word below:

SECURD	
SHORTN	
LISTSETH	
RESIDE	
HASNIB	
TAGNERM	
TENIMY	
FATCRY	
PRESENT	
DRAGU	

Write the definition for each word:

1. Crafty:

_____
_____
_____
_____
_____
_____

2. Serpent:

_____
_____
_____
_____
_____
_____

3. Enmity:

_____
_____
_____
_____
_____
_____

4. Thorns:

_____
_____
_____
_____
_____
_____

5. Guard:

_____
_____
_____
_____
_____
_____

6. Thistles:

_____
_____
_____
_____
_____
_____

7. Banish:

_____
_____
_____
_____
_____
_____

8. Desire:

_____
_____
_____
_____
_____
_____

9. Cursed:

_____
_____
_____
_____
_____
_____

10. Garment:

_____
_____
_____
_____
_____

Genesis Chapter 3

The fall of Man

1. Which animal did God make craftier then all the others?

   _____

   _____

   _____

   _____

2. What did the serpent ask Eve?

   _____

   _____

   _____

   _____

3. How did Eve respond to the serpent?

   _____

   _____

   _____

   _____

4. Go back to 2:16 & 17; did Eve or the serpent repeat God's commandment without adding or taking away from His word?

   Circle one: YES   NO

   a. Explain what the serpent added or took away from the Word of God?

   _____

   _____

   _____

   _____

   b. Explain what Eve added or took away from the Word of God?

   _____

   _____

   _____

   _____

5. There were two trees in the center of the Garden of Eden name each one:

   a. _____   b. _____

6. Which tree did God command Adam not to eat from?

_____
_____
_____
_____

7. Why did Eve eat from the tree of knowledge?

_____
_____
_____
_____

8. Did Eve eat from the tree of knowledge by herself?

_____
_____
_____
_____

    a. If not who did Eve give to eat after she ate?

_____
_____
_____

9. After eating from the tree what did Adam and Eve realize about themselves?

_____
_____
_____
_____

10. What did Adam and Eve use to cover their nakedness?

_____
_____
_____
_____

11. When did Adam and Eve hear the Lords' voice?

_____
_____
_____
_____

12. What did Adam and Eve do when they heard the voice of the Lord?

_____

_____

_____

_____

13. Did the Lord allow Adam and Eve to hide in shame?

Circle one: YES   NO

14. Why do you believe God called Adam and not Eve?

_____

_____

_____

_____

15. What did God ask Adam?

_____

_____

_____

_____

16. What was Adam's response?

_____

_____

_____

_____

17. Who did Adam blame for his disobedience to God?

_____

_____

_____

18. Who did Eve blame for her disobedience to God?

_____

_____

_____

19. Who did God blame for Adam and Eve's disobedience to His command?

_____

_____

_____

_____

20. What punishment did God pass down to those He blamed for this disobedience?

    a. The serpent:

        _____
        _____
        _____
        _____
        _____
        _____
        _____

    b. Eve:

        _____
        _____
        _____
        _____
        _____
        _____
        _____
        _____

    c. Adam:

        _____
        _____
        _____
        _____
        _____
        _____
        _____
        _____

21. Who does the Scripture state Eve was named the mother of?

22. How did God cover Adam and Eve's nakedness?

23. God had to remove Adam and Eve from the Garden of Eden for two reasons name the reasons and give the verse(s) that revealed these reasons to you.

a. _____
_____
_____
_____
_____
_____
_____
_____
_____

b. _____
_____
_____
_____
_____
_____
_____
_____
_____

24. What did God do after driving man out of the Garden and why?

_____
_____
_____
_____

Written Essay

There were two trees in the middle of the Garden of Eden; write a brief essay explaining why you believe the serpent chose the one he chose to get Eve to eat from; include why you feel this way:

_____
_____
_____
_____
_____
_____
_____
_____
_____
_____
_____
_____
_____
_____
_____
_____

GENESIS CHAPTER 4

Cain and Abel

Spelling/Definition words write each 3x each:

Downcast			
Crouching			
Restless			
Punishment			
Master			
Raise			
Avenge			
Injuring			
Suffer			
Wound			

Write each word in ABC order:

Downcast	
Crouching	
Restless	
Punishment	
Master	
Raise	
Avenge	
Injuring	
Suffer	
Wound	

Using your spelling words—unscramble each word below:

GAVENE	
SIRAE	
FREFUS	
GRINJINU	
CHUGNIRCO	
SHUNTPINME	
DUWON	
SERLSETS	
STACONDW	
STREAM	

Write the definition for each word:

1. Downcast:

_____
_____
_____
_____
_____
_____

2. Crouching:

_____
_____
_____
_____
_____
_____

3. Restless:

_____
_____
_____
_____
_____
_____

4. Punishment:

_____
_____
_____
_____
_____
_____

5. Master:

_____
_____
_____
_____
_____
_____

6. Raise:

_____
_____
_____
_____
_____
_____

7. Avenge:

_____
_____
_____
_____
_____
_____

8. Injuring:

_____
_____
_____
_____
_____
_____

9. Suffer:

_____
_____
_____
_____
_____
_____

10. Wound:

_____
_____
_____
_____
_____
_____

Genesis Chapter 4

Cain and Abel

1. Who had Adam laid with and what happened when he laid with her?

   _____

   _____

   _____

   _____

2. What did Eve say when she gave birth to her son?

   _____

   _____

   _____

   _____

3. Who did Eve give birth to later?

   _____

   _____

   _____

   _____

4. What were the jobs of Eve's two sons?

   a. _____   b. _____

5. In the course of time, what did Cain bring unto God?

   _____

   _____

   _____

   _____

6. In the course of time, what did Abel bring unto God?

   _____

   _____

   _____

7. How had the Lord looked on each of their offerings?

   _____

   _____

   _____

   _____

8. What did the Lord say to Cain?

_____
_____
_____
_____

9. What did Cain say to his brother Abel?

_____
_____
_____
_____

10. What happened while Cain and his brother were in the Field?

_____
_____
_____
_____

11. What did the Lord ask Cain concerning his brother Abel?

_____
_____
_____
_____

12. What was Cain's reply to the Lord?

_____
_____
_____
_____

13. What was the Lord's reply to Cain's answer concerning his brother Abel?

_____
_____
_____
_____

14. What was Cain's reply to the Lord concerning his punishment?

_____
_____
_____
_____

15. What did the Lord say to Cain concerning his feelings about his punishment?

_____
_____
_____
_____

16. Why did the Lord put a mark on Cain?

_____

_____

_____

_____

17. Where did Cain live when he went out from the Lord's presence?

_____

_____

_____

_____

18. What happened when Cain laid with his wife?

_____

_____

_____

_____

19. What was Cain building and what did he name it?

_____

_____

_____

_____

20. Who was born to Enoch?

_____

_____

_____

_____

21. Who was Mehujael the father of?

_____

_____

_____

_____

22. Who was Mathushael the father of?

_____

_____

_____

_____

23. How many wives did Lemech have and what were their names?

_____

_____

_____

_____

24. Who did Adah give birth to?

25. Who was Jabal the father of?

26. What was Jabal's brother name?

27. Who was Jubal the father of?

28. What was the name of Zillah's son and what did he do?

29. What was the name of Tubal-Cain's sister?

30. What did Lemech say to his two wives?

31. What happened when Adam laid with his wife again and what did his wife say when it happened?

_____

_____

_____

_____

32. What was the name of Seth's son?

_____

_____

_____

_____

33. What did men begin to do again, at that time?

_____

_____

_____

_____

Written Essay #1

After reading this text and seeing that God gave jobs to Cain and Able as young boys and expected them to make good offerings from their first fruits do you think God can and/or will use children today and expect the best from what He instruct them to do? Explain your answer:

_____

_____

_____

_____

_____

_____

_____

_____

_____

_____

_____

_____

_____

_____

_____

_____

_____

_____

_____

Written Essay #2

By reading this text we can see that God will speak to children. Do you believe God will speak to you and give you divine guidance and if so, will you listen for Him and how would you answer to His correction and/or directions? Explain your answer.

_____
_____
_____
_____
_____
_____
_____
_____
_____
_____
_____
_____
_____
_____
_____
_____
_____
_____
_____
_____
_____
_____
_____
_____
_____
_____
_____
_____
_____
_____
_____
_____
_____
_____
_____
_____

From Adam to Noah

Spelling/Definition words write each word 3xs each:

Genealogy			
Descendant			
Life			
Image			
Together			
Likeness			
Father			
Sibling			
Birth			
Mother			

Write each word in ABC order:

Genealogy	
Descendant	
Life	
Image	
Together	
Likeness	
Father	
Sibling	
Birth	
Mother	

Using your spelling words—unscramble each word below:

GETHERTO	
FILE	
BIGNILS	
REFHAT	
ROMEHT	
EMIGA	
HIRBT	
SETCANDEND	
YOGANEGEL	
LINESKES	

Write the definition for each word:

1. Genealogy:

2. Descendant:

3. Life:

4. Image:

5. Together:

6. Likeness:

_____
_____
_____
_____
_____
_____

7. Father:

_____
_____
_____
_____
_____
_____

8. Sibling:

_____
_____
_____
_____
_____
_____

9. Birth:

_____
_____
_____
_____
_____
_____

10. Mother:

_____
_____
_____
_____
_____
_____

Genesis Chapter 5

From Adam to Noah

Fill-in-the-Blanks

This is the _____ account of Adam's line. When God created man, he made him in the likeness of God. He created them male and female and blessed them. And when they were _____, he called them man. When Adam had lived 130 years, he had a son in his own _____; and he named him Seth. After Seth was born, Adam lived 800 years and had other sons and daughters. Altogether, Adam lived 930 years, and then he _____. When Seth had lived 105 years he became the father of Enosh. And after he became the father of Enosh, Seth lived _____ years and had other sons and daughters, _____, Seth lived 912 years and then he died. When Enosh had lived 90 years, he became the father of Kenan. And after he _____ the father of Kenan, Enosh lived 815 years, and then died. When Kenan had lived 70 years, he became the father of Mahalalel. And _____ he became the father of Mahalalel, Kenan lived 840 years and had other sons and daughters. Altogether, Kenan lived 910 years, and then he died. When _____ had lived 65 years, he became the father of _____. And after he became the father of Jared, Mahalalel lived _____ years and had other sons and daughters. Altogether, _____ lived 895 years, and then he died. When Jared had lived 162 years, he became the father of Enoch. And after he became the father of _____, Jared lived 800 years and had _____ sons and daughters. Altogether, Jared lived _____ years, and then he died. When Enoch had lived 65 years, he became the father of Methuselah. And after he became the father of _____, Enoch walked with God 300 years and had other sons and daughters. Altogether, Enoch lived 365 years. Enoch _____ with God; then he was no more because God took him _____. When Methuselah had lived 187 years, he became the father of _____. And after he became the father of Lamech, Methuselah lived 782 years and had other sons and daughters. Altogether, Methuselah lived 969 _____, and then he died. When Lamech had lived 182 years, he had a son. He named him Noah and said, "He will comfort us in the labor and _____ toil of our hands _____ by the ground the Lord has cursed. After Noah was born, Lamech lived 595 years and had other sons and daughters. Altogether, Lamech lived _____ years, and then he died. After Noah was 500 years old, he became the father of _____, _____ and _____.

Genesis Chapter 5

From Adam to Noah

1. Whose lineage does the writer state this is a written account of?

   _____
   _____
   _____
   _____

2. How does the text state God created man when He created them?

   _____
   _____
   _____
   _____

3. Give the written account of Adam:

   _____
   _____
   _____
   _____

4. Give the written account of Seth:

   _____
   _____
   _____
   _____

5. Give the written account of Enosh:

   _____
   _____
   _____
   _____

6. Give the written account of Kenan:

   _____
   _____
   _____
   _____

7. Give the written account of Mahalalel:

   _____
   _____
   _____
   _____

8. Give the written account of Jared:

_____
_____
_____
_____

9. Give the written account of Enoch:

_____
_____
_____
_____

10. Give the written account of Methuselah:

_____
_____
_____
_____

11. Give the written account of Lemech:

_____
_____
_____
_____

12. Who did Noah become the father of and when had he become the father of them?

_____
_____
_____
_____

Written Essay

Note the ages God allowed man to live in this biblical passage; then write a short paragraph on the differences in the amount of years God allow man to live now as compared to then and why you believe this is so and what Scripture(s) tell us the number of years a man shall live:

_____
_____
_____
_____
_____
_____
_____
_____
_____
_____
_____
_____
_____
_____
_____
_____
_____
_____
_____
_____
_____
_____
_____
_____
_____
_____
_____
_____
_____
_____
_____
_____
_____

The Flood

Spelling/Definition words write each word 3xs each:

Mortal			
Nephilim			
Wickedness			
Grieve			
Righteousness			
Corrupt			
Violence			
Pitch			
Store			
Covenant			

Write each word in ABC order:

Mortal	
Nephilim	
Wickedness	
Grieve	
Righteousness	
Corrupt	
Violence	
Pitch	
Store	
Covenant	

Using your spelling words—unscramble each word below:

RETSO	
PURTROC	
STONEHUGRISES	
HIPCT	
COILNEVE	
VOCENCANT	
LARMTO	
CWISESENDK	
MENLIPHI	
VIRGEE	

Write the definition for each word:

1. Mortal:

2. Nephilim:

3. Wickedness:

4. Grieve:

5. Righteousness:

6. Corrupt:

_____
_____
_____
_____
_____
_____

7. Violence:

_____
_____
_____
_____
_____
_____

8. Pitch:

_____
_____
_____
_____
_____
_____

9. Store:

_____
_____
_____
_____
_____
_____

10. Covenant:

_____
_____
_____
_____
_____
_____

Genesis Chapter 6

The Flood

1. What happened when men began to increase on the earth?

   _____

   _____

   _____

   _____

2. What did the Lord say concerning His Spirit?

   _____

   _____

   _____

   _____

3. When were the Nephilims on earth?

   _____

   _____

   _____

   _____

4. What were the Nephilims considered on earth?

   _____

   _____

   _____

   _____

5. What had the Lord seen on earth?

   _____

   _____

   _____

6. Why was the Lord grieved?

   _____

   _____

   _____

7. What did the Lord say concerning mankind?

   _____

   _____

   _____

   _____

8. What was the account of Noah?

_____

_____

_____

_____

9. What was the earth like at this time and who saw this happening on earth?

_____

_____

_____

_____

10. What did God say to Noah concerning the corruption on earth and what instruction had God given to Noah?

_____

_____

_____

_____

11. What did the Lord tell Noah to make himself?

_____

_____

_____

_____

12. What did the Lord instruct Noah to put in this he was to make for himself?

_____

_____

_____

_____

13. How did the Lord instruct Noah to build this ark?

_____

_____

_____

_____

14. Why did the Lord instruct Noah to build an ark?

_____

_____

_____

_____

15. What did the Lord state would perish?

_____

_____

_____

_____

16. What did the Lord state He would establish with Noah and who would enter into this ark Noah was to build?

_____

_____

_____

_____

17. What and who did the Lord instruct Noah to take into the ark?

_____

_____

_____

_____

18. What kind of food did the Lord instruct Noah to take into the ark with him?

_____

_____

_____

_____

19. Did Noah do everything God instructed him to do?

_____

_____

_____

_____

Written Essay #1

Write a brief essay explaining how this chapter can help you to understand that when God tells you to do something He gives instructions on how to do them, the importance of you following these instructions, and how many animals would have become extinct had Noah not followed God's instructions fully:

_____
_____
_____
_____
_____
_____
_____
_____
_____
_____
_____
_____
_____
_____
_____
_____
_____
_____
_____
_____
_____
_____
_____
_____
_____
_____
_____
_____
_____
_____
_____
_____
_____
_____
_____
_____
_____
_____

Rachel M. Sargent

Written Essay #2

Write a brief essay explaining everything God instructed Noah to take into the Ark include in your essay the measurements of the Ark and how life must have been back then to live in such close quarters with animals we consider wild and dangerous today:

_____
_____
_____
_____
_____
_____
_____
_____
_____
_____
_____
_____
_____
_____
_____
_____
_____
_____
_____
_____
_____
_____
_____
_____
_____
_____
_____
_____
_____
_____
_____
_____
_____
_____
_____

The Flood Continues

Spelling/Definition words write each word 3xs each:

Ark			
Mate			
Generation			
Escape			
Nostrils			
Male			
Female			
Pairs			
Enter			
Flood			

Write each word in ABC order:

Ark	
Mate	
Generation	
Escape	
Nostrils	
Male	
Female	
Pairs	
Enter	
Flood	

Using your spelling words—unscramble each word below:

LISTSORN	
PARIS	
NETER	
PEACES	
KAR	
TEAM	
TEARNONEGI	
DOFOL	
LAME	
LEAFME	

Write the definition for each word:

1. Ark:

_____
_____
_____
_____
_____
_____

2. Mate:

_____
_____
_____
_____
_____
_____

3. Generation:

_____
_____
_____
_____
_____
_____

4. Escape:

_____
_____
_____
_____
_____
_____

5. Nostrils:

_____
_____
_____
_____
_____
_____

6. Male:

_____
_____
_____
_____
_____
_____

7. Female:

_____
_____
_____
_____
_____
_____

8. Pairs:

_____
_____
_____
_____
_____
_____

9. Enter:

_____
_____
_____
_____
_____
_____

10. Flood:

_____
_____
_____
_____
_____
_____

Genesis Chapter 7

The Flood (cont.)

1. Why did God instruct Noah to take his family and go into the ark?

   _____

   _____

   _____

   _____

2. Did Noah listen to God's instructions?

   _____

   _____

   _____

   _____

3. How old was Noah when the floodwaters came to earth?

   _____

   _____

   _____

   _____

4. Who escaped the flood waters?

   _____

   _____

   _____

   _____

5. What animals came to Noah and entered the ark and who commanded these animals to do this?

   _____

   _____

   _____

   _____

6. When had the floodwaters come to earth?

   _____

   _____

   _____

7. When had the floodgates of heaven opened and what happened when they opened?

   _____

   _____

   _____

8. Who entered the ark and who commanded them to enter the ark?

9. Who shut the door to the ark?

10. What happened for forty days?

11. How does the writer describe the rain that fell upon the earth?

12. Who and what perished on earth?

13. What died on earth?

14. What was wiped out on earth?

15. Who was left on earth?

Written Essay

This chapter shows the wrath of God towards the sinful man. It also shows His mercy by allowing the righteous to live. Write a short paragraph explaining your feelings about the great floods and how this chapter can help us today.

_____

_____

_____

_____

_____

_____

_____

_____

_____

_____

_____

_____

_____

_____

_____

_____

_____

_____

_____

_____

_____

_____

_____

_____

_____

_____

_____

_____

_____

_____

_____

_____

_____

_____

_____

Chapter Review

Written Essays

Go back to the Scriptures stated below do a brief biblical/internet research; then write a synopsis of what happened at that time of the flood stated below:

7 days God shut the door of ark Genesis 7:7, 10, 16

40 days The flood begins Genesis 7:11

22 days Noah was 600 years old Genesis 7:11

The Flood Continues

Spelling/Definition words write each word 3xs each:

Recede			
Visible			
Inclination			
Cease			
Harvest			
Seedtime			
Curse			
Endure			
Surface			
Aroma			

Write each word in ABC order:

Recede	
Visible	
Inclination	
Cease	
Harvest	
Seedtime	
Curse	
Endure	
Surface	
Aroma	

Using your spelling words—unscramble each word below:

SEECA	
CASEFUR	
SUCER	
SMITEDEE	
NAILCOINTIN	
ROAMA	
ERUEND	
DEEREC	
LIVEBIS	
VERTSHA	

Write the definition for each word:

1. Recede:

    _____
    _____
    _____
    _____
    _____
    _____

2. Visible:

    _____
    _____
    _____
    _____
    _____
    _____

3. Inclination:

    _____
    _____
    _____
    _____
    _____
    _____

4. Cease:

    _____
    _____
    _____
    _____
    _____
    _____

5. Harvest:

    _____
    _____
    _____
    _____
    _____
    _____

6. Seedtime:

_____
_____
_____
_____
_____
_____

7. Curse:

_____
_____
_____
_____
_____
_____

8. Endure:

_____
_____
_____
_____
_____
_____

9. Surface:

_____
_____
_____
_____
_____
_____

10. Aroma:

_____
_____
_____
_____
_____
_____

Genesis Chapter 8

The Flood (cont.)

1. What had God remembered and what happened when he remembered this?

    _____

    _____

    _____

    _____

2. What had been closed and what happened when this was closed?

    _____

    _____

    _____

    _____

3. How does the text describe the way the waters receded upon the earth and when had the ark came to a rest?

    _____

    _____

    _____

    _____

4. How long had the waters continued to recede?

    _____

    _____

    _____

    _____

5. How did Noah send a raven out of the ark and what did the raven do when Noah sent this out of the Ark?

    _____

    _____

    _____

    _____

6. What did Noah send out of the ark next, what did this one that Noah sent out do and for how long did it do this?

    _____

    _____

    _____

    _____

7. How had Noah taken the dove back in?

_____

_____

_____

_____

8. How had Noah known the waters had receded?

_____

_____

_____

_____

9. How long did Noah wait to send the dove out again and did the dove return to the Ark?

_____

_____

_____

_____

10. When had the waters dried up from the earth?

_____

_____

_____

_____

11. What did Noah then remove and what did he see when he removed this?

_____

_____

_____

_____

12. When had the earth become completely dry?

_____

_____

_____

_____

13. What did God then say to Noah concerning him and those in the ark with him?

_____

_____

_____

_____

14. Did Noah do as God instructed him to do?

_____

_____

_____

_____

15. How had all come out of the ark?

    _____

    _____

    _____

    _____

16. What did Noah build when he came out of the Ark and what did he offer on it?

    _____

    _____

    _____

    _____

17. What did the aroma do to God and what did God say because of the aroma?

    _____

    _____

    _____

    _____

18. What eight things did God say will never cease as long as the earth endures?

    a. _____   e. _____

    b. _____   f. _____

    c. _____   g. _____

    d. _____   h. _____

Written Essay

Using the eight things God said would never cease as long as the earth endures; write a brief essay explaining how you can see these things in existence today and why it is necessary for them to exist as long as the earth endures.

_____

_____

_____

_____

_____

_____

_____

_____

_____

_____

_____

_____

Chapter Review

Written Essays

Go back to the Scriptures stated below do a brief biblical/internet research; then write a synopsis of what happened at that time of the flood stated below:

74 days Water goes down & the ark rest Genesis 8:1-4	_____

_____

40 days Mountain tops are seen Genesis 8:5-6	_____

_____

28 days Noah sends out birds Genesis 8:6-12	_____

_____

God's Covenant with Noah

Spelling/Definition words write each word 3xs each:

Fruitful			
Bloodshed			
Beast			
Earth			
Rainbow			
Everlasting			
Between			
Territory			
Extend			
Slave			

Write each word in ABC order:

Fruitful	
Bloodshed	
Beast	
Earth	
Rainbow	
Everlasting	
Between	
Territory	
Extend	
Slave	

Using your spelling words—unscramble each word below:

DENEXT	
RITETRYRO	
VELSA	
WENTEBE	
LOBEDHODS	
SEBAT	
OWBRAIN	
RUFFLUIT	
HEART	
STEALVINGER	

Write the definition for each word:

1. Fruitful:

    _____
    _____
    _____
    _____
    _____
    _____

2. Bloodshed:

    _____
    _____
    _____
    _____
    _____
    _____

3. Beast:

    _____
    _____
    _____
    _____
    _____
    _____

4. Earth:

    _____
    _____
    _____
    _____
    _____
    _____

5. Rainbow:

    _____
    _____
    _____
    _____
    _____
    _____

6. Everlasting:

_____
_____
_____
_____
_____
_____

7. Between:

_____
_____
_____
_____
_____
_____

8. Territory:

_____
_____
_____
_____
_____
_____

9. Extend:

_____
_____
_____
_____
_____
_____

10. Slave:

_____
_____
_____
_____
_____
_____

Genesis Chapter 9

Gods covenant with Noah/The Sons of Noah

Gods covenant with Noah

1. What did God say to bless Noah and his sons?

   _____
   _____
   _____
   _____

2. What did God say to Noah concerning what he must not eat?

   _____
   _____
   _____
   _____

3. What did God say to Noah concerning lifeblood?

   _____
   _____
   _____
   _____

4. What did God say to Noah concerning shedding blood in the land?

   _____
   _____
   _____
   _____

5. What did God state for Noah to do in the earth?

   _____
   _____
   _____
   _____

6. What did God say to Noah and his sons?

   _____
   _____
   _____
   _____

7. What covenant did God state he established with Noah?

   _____
   _____
   _____
   _____

8. What did God say to Noah concerning the sign of the covenant?

    _____

    _____

    _____

    _____

9. What had God said to Noah concerning who He established this covenant with?

    _____

    _____

    _____

    _____

The Sons of Noah

10. What were the names of the sons that came out of the ark with Noah?

    a. _____.   b. _____.   c. _____.

11. What nation was Ham the father of?

    _____

    _____

    _____

    _____

12. Who came from these three sons that came out of the ark with Noah?

    _____

    _____

    _____

    _____

13. What type of man does the text describe Noah to be and what did he do when he came out the ark?

    _____

    _____

    _____

    _____

14. Who saw their father's nakedness and what did he do when he saw this?

    _____

    _____

    _____

    _____

15. How did Shem and Japheth cover their father's nakedness?

_____

_____

_____

_____

16. When Noah awoke from his wine and found out what his youngest son had done what did he say?

_____

_____

_____

_____

17. How long had Noah lived after the flood and what age did he die?

_____

_____

_____

_____

Written Essay #1

Write a brief essay explaining which you believe was the right or wrong thing to have done when Ham saw his father's nakedness: exposing him to his brothers as Ham did or covering their father's nakedness as Shem and Japheth had done and why you feel this way:

_____

_____

_____

_____

_____

_____

_____

_____

_____

_____

_____

_____

_____

_____

_____

_____

_____

Written Essay #2

Note when Noah and all with him came out the ark; God gave him commands on what to eat and not to eat. Review Genesis chapter two; then write a brief essay explaining whom else God gave commands concerning what not to eat and what to eat; also relate the two covenants with the commands God give to us today as Christian's concerning what to and not to eat (take into our bodies) spiritually:

_____

_____

_____

_____

_____

_____

_____

_____

_____

_____

_____

_____

_____

_____

_____

_____

_____

_____

_____

_____

_____

_____

_____

_____

_____

_____

_____

_____

_____

_____

_____

_____

_____

_____

_____

_____

_____

_____

_____

The Table of Nations

Spelling/Definition write word each word 3xs each:

Japhethites			
Hamites			
Semites			
Clan			
Canaanites			
Territory			
Stretched			
Descent			
Region			
Warrior			

Write each word in ABC order:

Japhethites	
Hamites	
Semites	
Clan	
Canaanites	
Territory	
Stretched	
Descent	
Region	
Warrior	

Using your spelling words—unscramble each word below:

RITEROYTR	
GONIER	
SEEDTHCTR	
SCENTED	
RAWIROR	
PETSEATHIJH	
SITSEEM	
NALC	
ITSHAME	
TASINENACA	

Write the definition for each word:

1. Japhethites:

2. Hamites:

3. Semites:

4. Clan:

5. Canaanite:

6. Territory:

_____
_____
_____
_____
_____
_____

7. Stretched:

_____
_____
_____
_____
_____
_____

8. Descent:

_____
_____
_____
_____
_____
_____

9. Region:

_____
_____
_____
_____
_____
_____

10. Warrior:

_____
_____
_____
_____
_____
_____

Genesis Chapter 10

The Table of Nations

1. What were the names of Japheth's descendants?

_____
_____
_____
_____

2. What were the names of Ham's descendants?

_____
_____
_____
_____

3. What were the names of Shem's descendants?

_____
_____
_____
_____

4. What were the names of Canaan's descendants?

_____
_____
_____
_____

5. What were the names of Japheth's seven sons?

    a. _____   e. _____

    b. _____   f. _____

    c. _____   g. _____

    d. _____

6. What were the names of Gomer's three sons?

    a. _____   c. _____

    b. _____

7. What were the names of Javan's four sons?

    a. _____   c. _____

    b. _____   d. _____

8. What kind of people does the text state these people were?

_____

_____

_____

_____

9. Name the four sons of Ham?

a. _____   c. _____

b. _____   d. _____

10. Name the six sons of Cush?

a. _____   d. _____

b. _____   e. _____

c. _____   f. _____

11. Name the two sons of Raamah?

a. _____

b. _____

12. Which one of Cush son's grew up to be a warrior?

a. _____

13. What kind of warrior was he?

_____

_____

_____

_____

14. Where were the first centers of Nimrod's kingdom?

_____

_____

_____

_____

15. Name the five sons of Shem?

a. _____   d. _____

b. _____   e. _____

c. _____

16. Name the four sons of Aram?

       a. _____

       b. _____

       c. _____

       d. _____

17. Name the two sons of Eber?

       a. _____

       b. _____

18. Why was Peleg given this name?

_____

_____

_____

_____

19. Name the Thirteen sons of Joktan?

       a. _____   h. _____

       b. _____   i. _____

       c. _____   j. _____

       d. _____   k. _____

       e. _____   l. _____

       f. _____   m. _____

       g. _____

20. Where did Joktan and his thirteen sons dwell?

_____

_____

_____

_____

21. What happened to the Canaanites and how far did this nation reach?

_____

_____

_____

_____

22. Name the five sons of Shem?

      a. _____   d. _____

      b. _____   e. _____

      c. _____

23. Name Arphaxed's son?

      a. _____

24. Name Shelah's son?

      a. _____

25. Where did Nimrod build a city?

_____

_____

_____

_____

26. Name the seven nations Mizraim became the father of?

      a. _____

                           e. _____

      b. _____

                             f. _____

      c. _____

                             g. _____

      d. _____

27. Who was Canaan's first born son?

_____

_____

_____

_____

28. Name the eleven nations Canaan became the father of?

      a. _____   e. _____   i. _____

      b. _____   f. _____   j. _____

      c. _____   g. _____   k. _____

      d. _____   h. _____

Written Essay

Write a brief essay explaining how the generations has changed by the number of children each family had in the time this text was written and today:

_____
_____
_____
_____
_____
_____
_____
_____
_____
_____
_____
_____
_____
_____
_____
_____
_____
_____
_____
_____
_____
_____
_____
_____
_____
_____
_____
_____
_____
_____
_____
_____
_____
_____
_____
_____

Who am I?

Using the text as recorded in the Zondervan study bible; answer the following question to tell who is being spoken about in the descriptions below:

In the beginning was the word, and the word was with God; I am the Word. I am the only begotten Son to God Almighty. I am the Alpha and the Omega. I am the Prince of peace. I am the Heir of the Great "I Am", although I was first, I am the second Adam. I died on the cross, rose in three days, and ascended into heaven, seated on the right hand of God the Father, with all power in My hands. Every knee shall bow and every tongue shall confess I am Lord.

Who am I: _____

I killed a man for injuring me. I justified my sinful act by saying, "If Cain is avenged seven times for killing a man in a jealous rage; I am avenged seventy-seven times for killing a man in self-defense. I had two wives one named Adah and the other Zillah.

Who am I: _____

I was the son of God created in his image. I was created spirit man and became part flesh when God closed the place he opened me to take my rib and created my wife. I followed my wife instead of God and brought death into the world. I named all the animals. I was the first to live in the Garden of Eden. I gave the world a choice to follow God and live or follow the devil and die.

Who am I: _____

Although it never rained before I built an ark because the Lord instructed me to. The Lord was going to bring floodwaters to the earth to destroy all mankind and warned me of this. God started a whole new generation through me. My family and I stayed in the ark one hundred and ninety-seven days. My younger son saw me drunk and indecent and chose to expose me to his brothers, rather than, cover my naked drunken state and his son Canaan was cursed because of it.

Who am I: _____

God had mercy on my parents who were the first in the Garden of Eden, the first to sin, and the first to work the ground cursed by God. After one of my brothers was killed by the other the brother who killed him was thrown out of the Garden. Some years later God allowed my parents to have me. I began a whole new generation. My Generation went in the way of the Lord and my brother Cain's generation went in the way of the devil. It was detestable for our descendants to intermarry.

Who am I: _____

I became angry with my brother because God favored his offering. God spoke to me about my ways and how to change them but I did not listen and remained jealous and angry. I killed my brother and as a result God punished me by removing me from the Garden of Eden and cursed me to be a wanderer. I lived in the land of Nod, east of Eden, and I laid with my wife and she became pregnant and gave birth to Enoch. I built a city and called it Enoch.

Who am I: _____

We were in the ark with Noah. We are the two sons of Noah that loved and respected our father by covering him in his naked drunken state. One of us was the father of the Semites and the other was the father of the Japhethites.

Who are we: _____ and _____.

God closed my husband place that He opened to take his rib and create me with flesh. I was the first woman in the Garden of Eden. I was created because Adam was missing a help meet. I gave my husband a choice to follow me or follow God by offering him to eat of the tree of knowledge of good and evil that God commanded him not to eat. Our disobedience gave the whole world the choice to follow the Laws and Commands of God and live or follow the wiles of the devil and die.

Who am I: _____

I used words to trick Eve into eating from the tree of knowledge of good and evil that God commanded Adam not to eat from. I did this to take all that God gave man and deceive man to die. After I caused a lust in Eve's eye she helped me by getting Adam to eat from the tree of knowledge of good and evil. I was a dragon at this time then, God cursed me to crawl on my belly and put enmity between me and the woman.

Who am I: _____

My job from God was to maintain the flock. I brought God an offering from my first fruits. My brother Cain killed me because God favored my offering more than his and he became jealous. My blood cried out from the ground unto God and told Him what my brother did.

Who am I: _____

I saw my father drunk and naked and told my brothers, rather than, covering him. My son Canaan was cursed to be the slave of my brothers by my father for my sin against him. I was the father of the Hamites.

Who am I: _____

<u>*Genesis Chapter 1-10 Review*</u>

<u>*Part I: Written Essay*</u>

Go back to the Scriptures stated below do a brief biblical/internet research; then write a synopsis of what happened at that time of the flood:

110 days
Water covers
all the Earth
Genesis
7:17 & 8:1

_____

57 days
Noah Opens
the Roof
Genesis
8:13-19

_____

A New Start

Genesis
8:20 – 9:17

_____

Part II. Biblical Background

Give a brief synopsis explaining all that was done by God on each day as written in chapters 1 &
2 of the Zondervan NIV Study Bible:

The Days of Creation	
Day 1:	
Day 2:	
Day 3:	
Day 4:	
Day 5:	
Day 6:	
Day 7:	

Part III. Historical Research

Using your Zondervan Study Bible list some of the well-known people and events in the Old Testament from Genesis chapters 1-10 then write a brief synopsis of why they are known and accurately recorded in the Bible:

Well Known people in the Bible Genesis chapters 1-10	
Well known person:	**Brief synopsis:**

Well Known Events in the Bible Genesis chapters 1-10	
Well known events:	**Brief synopsis:**

Part IV. Biblical Remembrance

Name the 39 Books of the Old Testament in the order which they were written then name each by category given a brief synopsis why they were accurately recorded:

1. _____	14. _____	27. _____
2. _____	15. _____	28. _____
3. _____	16. _____	29. _____
4. _____	17. _____	30. _____
5. _____	18. _____	31. _____
6. _____	19. _____	32. _____
7. _____	20. _____	33. _____
8. _____	21. _____	34. _____
9. _____	22. _____	35. _____
10. _____	23. _____	36. _____
11. _____	24. _____	37. _____
12. _____	25. _____	38. _____
13. _____	26. _____	39. _____

List the five books of Law/Pentateuch:

Give a brief synopsis of why these five books of Law/Pentateuch were accurately recorded:

1. _____
2. _____
3. _____
4. _____
5. _____

List the twelve books of History:

Give a brief synopsis of why these twelve books of history were accurately recorded:

1. _____
2. _____
3. _____
4. _____
5. _____
6. _____
7. _____
8. _____
9. _____
10. _____
11. _____
12. _____

List the first five books of Major Prophets:

	Give a brief synopsis of why these five books of major prophets were accurately recorded:
1. _____	_____
2. _____	_____
3. _____	_____
4. _____	_____
5. _____	_____

List the next twelve books of Minor Prophets:

	Give a brief synopsis of why these five books of minor prophets were accurately recorded:
1. _____	_____
2. _____	_____
3. _____	_____
4. _____	_____
5. _____	_____
6. _____	_____
7. _____	_____
8. _____	_____
9. _____	_____
10. _____	_____
11. _____	_____
12. _____	_____

List the five books of Poetry:

	Give a brief synopsis of why these five books of poetry/wisdom were accurately recorded:
1. _____	_____
2. _____	_____
3. _____	_____
4. _____	_____
5. _____	_____

Name each book and division of the book of Psalms accurately recorded:

Book 1: _____

Book 2: _____

Book 3: _____

Book 4: _____

Book 5: _____

Genesis Chapter 1

The Beginning

ABC ORDER	SPELLING DEFINITIONS
Created	To bring into being; to give rise to; to produce; to invest with an office or title; appoint; to produce through artistic or imaginative effort; created.
Expanse	To spread out; a wide open extent.
Formless	Have no specified form; shapeless; lacking order.
Hovering	To remain floating or suspended in the air over a particular place; to stay or linger in or near a place; to be in a state of uncertainty or suspense; waver; an act or instance of hovering.
Image	A reproduction of a person or object, esp. a sculptured likeness; an optically or electronically formed duplicate or other representative reproduction; of an object, esp. an optical reproduction formed by a mirror or lens; a close or exact resemblance to another; double; the idea of someone or something that is held by the public; the character projected by someone or something to the public, esp. by the mass media; reputation; a personification of something specified; a mental picture of something unreal or not present; a vivid description or representation; a figure of speech; an apparition; a set of values of a function corresponding to a particular subset of a domain; an exact replica of the contents of a storage device, such as a hard disk, stored on a second storage device, such as a network server; to make a likeness of; to reflect; to symbolize or typify; to picture mentally; imagine; to describe, esp. to describe so vividly as to call up a mental picture of; to print a file using a laser printer, direct-to-plate press, or similar device; to transmit an exact replica of the contents of a storage device to another storage device; to render visually, as by magnetic resonance imaging.
Livestock	Domestic animals kept for use on a farm or raise for sale and profit.
Produce	To bring forth; yield; to create by physical or mental effort; to manufacture; to give rise to; to bring forward; exhibit; to sponsor and present to the public; to extend an area or volume or lengthen a line; to make or yield the customary product or products; a product, esp. farm products as a whole.

Separated	To set or keep apart; disunite; to scatter; to sort; to discriminate or differentiate between; distinguish; to extract from a mixture or combination; isolate; to part a married couple, usu. by decree; to discharge, as from employment or military service; to become disunited or severed; to withdraw; secede; to part company; disperse; to discontinue living together as husband and wife; to become divided into parts or components; set apart from others; detached; withdrawn from others; alone; existing by itself; independent; not alike; dissimilar; not shared; individual; a garment, as a skirt, jacket, or pair of slacks, designed to be worn in various combinations with other garments.
Surface	The exterior face of an object; a material layer constituting such an exterior face; the boundary of a three-dimensional figure; a portion of space having length and breadth but no thickness; superficial or outward appearance; as airfoil; relating to, on, or at a surface; relating to or occurring on or near the surface of the earth; superficial; merely apparent as opposed to real; to form the surface of, as by smoothing or leveling; to provide with a surface; to rise to the surface; to emerge after concealment.
Teem	To be full of; swarm; to be or become pregnant; produce young; to give birth to; to pour out or empty.

Unscramble Words:
Surface
Expanse
Teem
Image
Hovering
Formless
Separated
Created
Produce
Livestock

Genesis Chapter 1

The Beginning

1. In the beginning God created the heavens and the earth. Now the earth was formless and empty, darkness was over the surface of the deep.

2. The Spirit of God was hovering over the waters.

3. And God said, "Let there be light," and there was light.

4. God saw that the light was good, and he separated the light from darkness.

5. God called the light "day," and the darkness he called "night." And there was evening, and there was morning the first day.

6. God said, "Let there be an expanse between the waters to separate water from water."

7. God made the expanse and separated the water under the expanse from the water above it. And it was so.

8. God called the expanse "sky."

9. And there was evening, and there was morning the second day.

10. God said, "Let the water under the sky be gathered to one place, and let dry ground appear." And it was so.

11. God called the dry ground "land," and the gathered waters he called "seas." And God saw that it was good.

12. Then God said, "Let the land produce vegetation: seed-bearing plants and trees on the land that bear fruit with seed in it, according to their various kinds and it was so.

13. The land produced vegetation: plants bearing seed according to their kinds and trees bearing fruit with seed in it according to their kinds.

14. God saw that it was good and there was evening and there was morning the third day.

15. God said, "Let there be light in the expanse of the sky to separate the day from the night, and let them serve as signs to mark seasons and days and years and let them be lights in the expanse of the sky to give light on the earth." And it was so.

16. God made two great lights; the greater light to govern the day and the lesser light to govern the night.

17. God also made the stars and set them in the sky to give light on the earth, to govern the day and the night, and to separate light from darkness. And God saw that it was good.

18. There was evening, and there was morning the fourth day.

19. God said, "Let the water teem with living creatures, and let birds fly above the earth across the expanse of the sky.

20. So God created the great creatures of the sea and every living and moving thing with which the water teems, according to their kinds, and every winged bird according to its kind. And God saw that it was good.

21. God blessed them and said, "Be fruitful and increase in number and fill the water in the seas, and let the birds increase on the earth."

22. There was evening, and there was morning the fifth day.

23. God said, "Let the land produce living creatures according to their kinds: livestock, creatures that move along the ground, and wild animals, each according to their kinds, the livestock according to their kinds, and all the creatures that move along the ground according to their kinds and God saw that it was good.

24. Then God said, "Let us make man in our image, in our likeness, and let them rule over the fish of the sea and the birds of the air, over the livestock, over all the earth, and over all the creatures that move along the ground."

25. So God created man in His own image, in the image of God He created him: male and female He created them.

26. God blessed them and said to them, "Be fruitful and increase in number; fill the earth and subdue it. Rule over the fish of the sea and the birds of the air and over every living creature that moves on the ground."

27. God said, "I give you every seed-bearing plant on the face of the whole earth and every tree that has fruit with seed in it. They will be yours for food. And to all the beasts of the earth and all the birds of the air and all the creatures that move on the ground everything that has the breath of life in it I give every green plant for food." And it was so.

28. God saw all that He had made and it was very good.

29. There was evening and morning the sixth day.

Essay #1—Optional/Opinionated

Essay#2—Optional/Opinionated

Genesis Chapter 2

Adam and Eve

ABC ORDER	SPELLING DEFINITIONS
Account	A narrative or record of events; a reason given for a particular action or event; a report relating to one's conduct; a basis; ground; a business relationship involving the exchange of money or credit; a precise list or enumeration of financial transactions; money deposited for checking, savings, or brokerage use; a customer having a business or credit relationship with a firm; worth or importance; profit or advantage; to consider or esteem; to make or render a reckoning; to be the explanation or cause of; to be answerable for; to challenge or contest; to hold answerable for; to act in a creditable way; because of; under no circumstances; on one's own behalf; on one's own; by oneself; to take into consideration; the bookkeeping methods involved in making a financial record of business transactions and in the preparation of statements concerning the assets, liabilities, and operating results of a business.
Array	To arrange or draw up, as troop as in battle order; to clothe in finer; adorn; an orderly arrangement, esp. of troops; an impressive display of numerous persons or objects; splendid attire; finery; rectangular arrangement of quantities in rows and columns, as in matrix; numerical data linearly ordered by magnitude; an arrangement of computer memory elements in one or several plains.
Command	To give orders to; direct; to have authoritative control over; rule; to have at one's disposal; to deserve and receive as due; to give commands; to be in control; the act of commanding; an authoritative order or direction; a signal that activates a device, as a computer; the authority to command; the possession and exercise of authority to command; natural or acquired facility or skill; mastery; domination by position; the jurisdiction of a commander; a military unit, post, district or territory under the control of one officer; a unit in the US Air Force having a specified number of wings, generally three or more, under the authority of an officer; an invitation from a reigning monarch.
Evil	Morally wrong or bad; wicked; causing injury, ruin, or pain; harmful; marked by or indicating future misfortune; ominous; reputedly bad or blameworthy; infamous; a cause of harm, misfortune, or destruction; something morally reprehensible; wickedness; an evil power or force; a source or cause of suffering, harm, or destruction; in an evil manner.

Good	Having desirable or positive qualities; serving the desired end; suitable; not ruined or spoiled; being in excellent condition; better than average; designating the US Government grade of meat higher than standard and lower than choice; of high quality; handsome; attractive; beneficial; salutary; skilled; safe; sure; valid or true; real genuine; ample; enjoyable pleasant; of moral excellence; upright; well-behaved; passing between the uprights of the goal and therefore scoring.
Seed	A fertilized and ripened plant ovule having an embryo that is capable of germinating to produce a new plant; a beginning or source; origin; offspring; descendants; family stock; ancestry; sperm; semen; a small amount of material used to initiate a chemical reaction; a small crystal added to a solution to initiate crystallization; a pellet filled with a radioactive isotope that is implanted at the site of a cancerous tumor to provide localized administration of radiation; a young oyster or oysters used for propagating a new oyster bed; a competitor who has been ranked in a tournament; to plant seeds in; sow; to plant in soil; to remove the seeds from fruit; to furnish with something that grows or stimulates growth or development; to sprinkle a cloud with particles, as of silver iodide, in order to disperse it or induce rain; to arrange the drawing for positions in a tournament; to sow seed; to go to seed; to progress to the seed-bearing stage; to become useless or devitalized; deteriorate.
Shame	A painful feeling brought about by a strong sense of guilt, embarrassment, unworthiness, or disgrace; capacity for such a feeling; one that brings dishonor, disgrace, or condemnation; dishonor or disgrace; ignominy; a major disappointment; to cause to feel shame; to bring dishonor or disgrace on; to force by making ashamed; to fill with shame; disgrace; to outdo completely; surpass.
Suitable	That which is appropriate to a given purpose; fitting; appropriate; applicable; agreeable; becoming; as, language suitable to the subject.
United	To bring together so as to form a whole; to bring together by a common interest, attitude, or action; to join a couple in marriage; to cause to adhere; to have or exhibit qualities in combination; to become or seem to become joined, formed, or combined into a unit; to join and act together in a common purpose or endeavor; to be or become bound together by adhesion.
Vast	Very great in size, number amount, or quantity; very great in area or extent; immense; very great in degree or intensity; an immense space.

Unscrambled Words:
Vast
Shame
Evil
Array
Good
Account
Suitable
United
Seed
Command

Genesis Chapter 2

The Beginning (cont.)/Adam and Eve

The Beginning (cont.)

1. Thus the heavens and the earth were completed and their vast array.

2. By the seventh day God had finished the work He had been doing so on the seventh day He rested from all his work.

3. God blessed the seventh day and made it holy, because on it He rested from all the work of creating that He had done.

Adam and Eve

4. This is the account of the heavens and the earth when they were created.

5. When the Lord God made the earth and the heavens and no shrub of the field had yet appeared on the earth and no plant of the field had yet sprung up, for the Lord God had not sent rain on the earth and there was no man to work the ground, but streams came up from the ground the Lord God formed the man from the dust of the ground and breath into his nostrils the breath of life, and the man became a living being.

6. The Lord God had planted a garden in the east, in Eden.

7. There in the east of Eden where God planted the garden He put the man he had formed.

8. The Lord God made all kinds of trees grow out of the ground; trees that were pleasing to the eye and good for food.

9. The tree of life and the tree of the knowledge knowing good and evil were in the middle of the garden.

10. A river watering the garden flowed from Eden; from there it was separated into four waterheads.

11. The name of the first waterhead was Pishon; it winds through the entire land of Havilah, where there is gold.

12. The gold of that land is good; aromatic resin and onyx are also there.

13. The name of the second waterhead was Gihon; it winds through the entire land of Cush.

14. The name of the third waterhead was Tigris; it runs along the east side of Asshur.

15. The name of the fourth waterhead was the Euphrates.

16. The Lord God took the man and put him in the Garden of Eden to work it and take care of it.

17. The Lord God commanded the man, "You are free to eat from any tree in the garden; but you must not eat from the tree of the knowledge knowing good and evil, for when you eat of it you will surely die."

18. The Lord God said, "It is not good for man to be alone. I will make a helper suitable for him."

19. The Lord God formed out of the ground all the beasts of the field and all the birds of the air and brought them to the man to see what he would name them; whatever the man called each living creature, that was its name. So the man gave names to all the livestock, the birds of the air and all the beasts of the field.

20. For Adam no suitable helper was found. And as a result the Lord God caused the man to fall into a deep sleep; and while he was sleeping, he took one of the man's ribs and closed up the place with flesh.

21. Then the Lord God made a woman from the rib He had taken out of the man, and He brought her to the man.

22. When God brought the woman to Adam, Adam said: "This is now bone of my bones and flesh of my flesh; she shall be called 'woman.' For she was taken out of man."

23. For this reason a man will leave his father and mother and be united to his wife, and they will become one flesh.

24. The man and his wife were both naked, and they felt no shame.

Genesis Chapter 3

The fall of Man

ABC ORDER	SPELLING DEFINITIONS
Banish	To force to leave a country or place by official decree; exile; to drive away expel.
Crafty	Skillfully underhand and deceptive shrewd; ingenious; skillful.
Cursed	An appeal for evil or injury to befall someone or something; evil or injury resulting from or as if from an invocation; one that is accursed; something bringing or causing evil; scourge; a profane oath; an ecclesiastical censor, ban, or anathema; menstruation; to invoke evil, calamity, or injury upon; damn; to swear at; to bring evil upon; afflict; to put under an ecclesiastical ban or anathema; excommunicate; to utter curses; swear; that deserves to be cursed; wicked.
Desire	To wish or long for; crave; to express a wish for; request; a wish, longing, or craving; a request or petition; one that is longed for; sexual appetite; passion.
Enmity	The attitude or feelings of an enemy or enemies; hostility; antagonism; deep rooted mutual hatred.
Garment	Any article of clothing; a covering; to cover with a garment; to clothe.
Guard	To shield from danger or harm, esp. by careful prevent escape, violence, or indiscretion; to keep watch at a door to supervise entries and exits; to keep a player on an opposing team from scoring or playing effectively; to furnish a device or object with a protective piece; to escort; to take precautions; to serve as a guard; one that acts as a sentinel or stands watch; one who supervises prisoners; a body of ceremonial occasions; a railway employee in charge of a train; one of the two players who initiate plays from the center of the court; a defensive position or stance in certain sports; the act or duty of guarding; protection; watch; an injury, damage, or loss, esp. and attachment or voce ring put on a machine to protect the operator; a chain or band for safeguarding something, as a bracelet, from loss; a ring for preventing a more valuable ring from sliding off the finger; a signal that prevents accidental activation of a device or ambiguous interpretation of data.
Serpent	Revelations 12:9 & 20:2 tells us the serpent of ancient times, spoken of in this chapter was that of a dragon not a snake until cursed by God to crawl on its belly. Webster's description of a serpent: the creature that tempted Eve in the Garden of Eden; the devil; one who is subtle, sly, or treacherous; a firework that twists and turns while burning; a deep-voiced 18th century wind instrument of serpentine shape, approx. eight feet long and made of brass or wood.
Thistles	Any of numerous Onopordum, with prickly leaves and usu. purplish flowers surrounded by prickly bracts; a plant similar or related to a thistle.

Thorn	A modified branch in the form of a sharp woody spine; a shrub, tree, or woody plant bearing causes sharp pain, irritation, or discomfort; the runic letter "Þ" orig. representing either sound of the Modern English "th", as in the and thin, used in Old English and Middle English manuscripts.

Unscrambled Words:
Cursed
Thorns
Thistles
Desire
Banish
Garment
Enmity
Crafty
Serpent
Guard

Genesis Chapter 3

The fall of Man

1. The serpent was craftier than any of the wild animals God had made

2. The serpent said to the woman, "Did God really say, 'You must not eat from any tree in the Garden?'"

3. The woman said to the serpent, "We may eat fruit from the trees in the garden, but God did say; "you must not eat fruit from the tree that is in the middle of the garden, and you must not touch it, or you will die.'

4. No; neither the serpent nor Eve repeated exactly what God said to Adam.

    a. The serpent completely changed God's words by saying they could not eat from any tree. The fruits of the trees were what God gave them to eat and the serpent knew this his choice words were to get Eve to sin.

    b. Eve added that God said: "The tree in the middle of the Garden you must not eat or you must not touch it. God specifically said the tree of knowledge knowing good and evil and He did not say anything about touching the tree. It is important to note that God specifically said the tree of knowledge knowing good and evil because there were two trees in the middle of the garden and had Eve of ate from the tree of life instead of the tree of knowledge knowing good and evil it would have had a different outcome.

5. The tree of life and the tree of knowledge knowing good and evil.

6. God told them not to eat from the tree of knowledge knowing good and evil.

7. When Eve saw that the fruit of the tree was good for food and pleasing to the eye, and desirable for gaining wisdom she ate the fruit of the tree of knowledge knowing good and evil.

8. No, Eve did not eat of the fruit alone.

    a. Eve also gave to her husband Adam to eat.

9. After eating the fruit Adam and Eve realized that they were naked.

10. Adam and Eve sewed fig leaves together to cover their nakedness.

11. Adam and Eve heard the Lords voice while walking in the Garden in the cool of the day.

12. When Adam and Eve heard the Lords voice they hid themselves.

13. No, God did not allow Adam and Eve to hide in their shame.

14. Opinionated question—should use Scripture to support your answer.

15. God asked Adam, "Where are you?"

16. Adam replied; "I heard you in the Garden, and I was afraid because I was naked; so I hid."

17. Adam blamed Eve for disobeying God.

18. Eve blamed the serpent for disobeying God.

19. God blamed all three starting with the serpent.

20. God punished each accordingly:

    a. To the serpent He said, "Cursed are you above all the livestock and all the wild animals! You will crawl on your belly and you will eat dust all the days of your life, and I will put enmity between you and the woman, and between your offspring and hers; he will crush your head and you will strike his heel."

    b. To the woman He said, "I will greatly increase your pains in childbearing: with pain you will give birth to children. Your desire will be for your husband, and he will rule over you."

    c. To Adam He said; "Because you listened to your wife and ate from the tree about which I commanded you. 'You must not eat of it, "cursed is the ground because of you; through painful toil you will eat of it all the days of your life. It will produce thorns and thistles for you and you will eat the plants of the field. By the sweat of your brow you will eat your food until you return to the ground. Since from it you were taken, for dust you are and to dust you will return."

21. Eve was named the mother of all the living.

22. The Lord made garments of skin for Adam and his wife and clothed them.

23. God had to remove Adam and Eve from the Garden for the following reasons:

    a. They sinned and disobeyed his commandment. They had become like God knowing good and evil. (vs. 22)

    b. Because they disobeyed Gods commandment, they had to die and God had to see to it that they would not be able to eat from the tree of life (vs. 22)

24. After God drove the man out, He placed on the east side of the Garden of Eden cherubim and a flaming sword flashing back and forth to guard the way to the tree of life.

Genesis Chapter 4

Cain and Able

ABC ORDER	SPELLING DEFINITIONS
Avenge	To get revenge for a wrong, injury, etc. by punishing the injuring party; to take vengeance on behalf of, as for a wrong; to exact revenge or satisfaction for; to take vengeance on behalf of.
Crouching	To stoop with the legs pulled close to the body; to cringe in a servile way; to cause to bend low, as in humility or fear.
Downcast	A casting down; sadness; melancholy look; directed downward; low in spirit.
Injuring	Damage of or to a person, property, reputation, or thing; a wound or other specific damage; a wrong or damage done to a person or to his or her property, reputation, or rights when caused by the wrongful act of another; an insult.
Master	One with control over the actions of another or others; the captain of a merchant ship; one who employs an apprentice; an employee; the owner or keeper of an animal; the owner of a slave; the head of a household; one who has control over something; possessor; one who defeats another; a teacher, schoolmaster, or tutor; one whose teachings or doctrines are accepted by followers; Christianity, Jesus; a learned person; scholar; one who holds a master's degree; an artist or teach an apprentices; an expert; a title once read for a man holding a naval office ranking next below a lieutenant on a warship; the title of the head or presiding officer of certain societies, clubs, orders, or institutions; the title of various law court officers; the title of any of various officers with specified duties involving the management of the British royal household; a person who owns a pack of hounds or is a chief officer of a hunt; a form of address for a man; mister; an original from which copies can be made; being something specified in a superlative degree; highly skilled; expert; controlling all other parts of a mechanism;

	being an original from which copies are made; to act as or be the master; to make oneself a master of; to overcome or defeat, as an addiction; to break or tame a person or animal or defeat, as an addiction; to break or tame a person or animal; subjugate; to season or age dyed goods.
Punishment	An act of punishing or the state of being punished; a penalty imposed for wrongdoing; rough handling; to subject someone to a penalty for a crime, fault, or bad behavior; to inflict a penalty on a wrongdoer for an offense; to handle harshly; injure; to deplete a stock or supply heavily; to give punishment.
Raise	To move or cause to move upward or to a higher position; lift; to set or place upright; stand; to build or erect; to cause to appear, arise, or exist; to awaken from or as if from death; to increase in quantity, size, or worth; to increase in intensity, strength, degree, or pitch; to improve in rank or dignity; promote; to bring up; rear; to accustom to something from an early age; to put forward for consideration; to begin or set a lawsuit in operation; to utter or express a cry; to bring about; to gather together; collect; to cause dough to rise; to end a siege by withdrawing troops or forcing the enemy troops to withdraw; to remove or withdraw an order; to increase; to bet more than a preceding bettor; to increase stakes; to bring into sight by approaching nearer; to alter and increase illegally the written value of a check; to cough up phlegm; to make angry; enrage; to make contact with esp. by radio; to increase the stakes; an act of raising or increasing; an increase in wages; to behave in a rowdy or disruptive way; to reprimand someone severely and loudly; to cause surprise, amazement, or consternation.
Restless	Without quiet, repose, or rest; unable to rest, relax or be still; constantly in motion.
Suffer	To feel experience or endure pain or distress; to sustain loss, injury, harm, or punishment; to appear at a disadvantage; to undergo or sustain pain, injury, or unpleasantness; to experience a change in staffing; to endure; bear; to permit; allow.
Wound	An injury to the body in which the skin or other tissue is broken, cut, pierced, torn, etc.

Unscrambled Words:
Avenge
Raise
Suffer
Injuring
Crouching
Punishment
Wound
Restless
Downcast
Master

Genesis Chapter 4

Cain and Able

1. Adam laid with his wife Eve, and she became pregnant and gave birth to Cain.

2. She said, "With the help of the Lord I have brought forth a man."

3. Later Eve gave birth to his brother Abel.

4. Abel kept flocks and Cain worked the soil.

5. In the course of time Cain brought some of the fruits of the soil as an offering to the Lord.

6. In that course of time, Abel brought fat portions from some of the firstborn of his flock.

7. The Lord looked with favor on Abel and his offering, but on Cain and his offering he did not, look with favor and Cain was very angry and his face was downcast.

8. Then the Lord said to Cain, "Why are you angry? Why is your face downcast? If you do what is right, will you not be accepted? But if you do not do what is right, sin is crouching at your door; it desires to have you, but you must master it."

9. Cain said to his brother Abel, "Let's go out to the field."

10. While they were in the field, Cain attacked his brother Abel and killed him.

11. Then the Lord said to Cain, "Where is your brother Abel."

12. "I don't know," he replied. "Am I my brother's keeper?"

13. The Lord said, "What have you done? Listen! Your brother's blood cries out to me from the ground. Now you are under a curse and driven from the ground, which opened its mouth to receive your brothers' blood from your hand. When you work the ground, it will no longer yield its crops for you. You will be a restless wanderer on the earth."

14. Cain said to the Lord concerning his punishment, "My punishment is more than I can bear. Today you are driving me from the land, and I will be hidden from your presence; I will be a restless wanderer on the earth, and whoever finds me will kill me."

15. But, the Lord said to him, "Not so; if anyone kills Cain, he will suffer vengeance seven times over."

16. Then the Lord put a mark on Cain so that no one who found him would kill him.

17. Cain went out from the Lord's presence and lived in the land of Nod, east of Eden.

18. Cain laid with his wife and she became pregnant and gave birth to Enoch.

19. Cain was then building a city, and he named it after his son Enoch.

20. To Enoch was born Irad and Irad was the father of Mehujael.

21. Mehujael was the father of Mathushael.

22. Mathushael was the father of Lamech.

23. Lamech married two women; one named Adah and the other Zillah.

24. Adah gave birth to Jabal.

25. Jabal was the father of those who live in tents and raised livestock.

26. His brother's name was Jubal.

27. Jubal was the father of all who played the harp and flute.

28. Zillah also had a son name Tubal-Cain who forged all kinds of tools out of bronze and iron.

29. Tubal-Cain's sister was Naamah.

30. Lemech said to his two wives, "Adah and Zillah, listen to me; wives of Lamech, hear my words. I have killed a man for wounding me, a young man for injuring me. If Cain is avenged seven times, then Lemech seventy-seven times.

31. Adam lay with his wife again, and she gave birth to a son and named him Seth, saying, "God has granted me another child in place of Abel, since Cain killed him."

32. Seth also had a son and he named him Enosh.

33. At that time men began to call on the name of the Lord.

Genesis Chapter 5

From Adam to Noah

ABC ORDER	SPELLING DEFINITIONS
Birth	The beginning of existence; the fact of being born; a beginning; origin; the act of bearing young; parturition; passage of a child from the uterus; ancestry; parentage; origin; lineage; to deliver a baby; to bear a child; to bring into being.
Descendant	An individual descended from an ancestor in any degree; offspring of a certain ancestor, family, group, etc.; something derived from an earlier form or prototype.

Father	A male parent of a child; forefather; a man who creates or originates something; the first person of the Trinity; an old venerable man; a member of the ancient Roman senate; any of various authoritative early writers in the Christian church who formulated doctrines and codified religious observances; a priest or clergyman in the Roman Catholic, Anglican, or Eastern Orthodox churches; to procreate offspring as the male parent; to act or serve as a father to; to create, found, or originate; to acknowledge responsibility for; to attribute the paternity, creation, or origin of; to assign falsely or unjustly; foist; to act or serve as a father.
Genealogy	A record or table of familial descent; direct descent from an ancestor; lineage; the study of family histories.
Image	A reproduction of a person or object, esp. a sculptured likeness; an optically or electronically formed duplicate or other representative reproduction of an object, esp. an optical reproduction formed by a mirror or lens; a close or exact resemblance to another; double; the idea of someone or something that is held by the public; the character projected by someone or something to the public, esp. by the mass media; reputation; a personification of something specified; a mental picture of something unreal or not present; a vivid description or representation; a figure of speech; an apparition; a set of values of a function corresponding to a particular subset of a domain; to make a likeness of; to reflect; to symbolize or typify; to picture mentally; imagine; to describe, esp. to describe so vividly as to call up a mental picture of; to print a file using a laser printer, direct-to-plate press or similar device to transmit an exact replica of the contents of a storage device to another storage device; to render visually, as by magnetic resonance imaging.
Life	The property or quality distinguishing living organisms from dead organisms and inanimate matter, manifested in functions such as growth, metabolism, response to stimuli, and reproduction; living organisms as a whole; a living being, esp. a person; the physical, mental, and spiritual experiences that constitute a person existence; the interval of time; a particular segment of this period; the period of time between one's birth and the present; the period from an occurrence until death; the time for which something functions or exists; a spiritual state regarded as a transcending of death; an account of a person's life; human existence or activity; a manner of living; the activities and interest of a particular area or realm; a source of vitality; animating force; liveliness or vitality; animation; something that actually exists regarded as a subject for an artist; actual environment or reality; nature; necessary for or involved in living; continuing for a lifetime; lifelong.
Likeness	Resembling to another; an imitative appearance; semblance; an artistic representation; image.

Mother	A female parent; a woman holding an authoritative or responsible position similar to that of a mother; a creative source; origin; an elderly or old woman; qualities attributed to a mother, as capacity to love; the biggest or most significant example of its kind; to give birth to; be the mother of; to create; produce; to watch over, nourish, and protect; to act or serve as a mother; a stringy slime of yeast cells and bacteria that form on the surface of fermenting liquids and is added to wine or cider to start production of vinegar.
Sibling	One of two or more persons having one or both parents in common.
Together	In or into a single mass, group, or place; in relationship, one to another; mutually or reciprocally; regarded collectively; at once; simultaneously; in accord or harmony; in an effective, coherent condition; being in tune with what is going on; unified and performing effectively; to unify, harmonize, and integrate one's resources so as to perform with top effectiveness.

Unscrambled Words:
Together
Life
Sibling
Father
Mother
Image
Birth
Descendant
Genealogy
Likeness

Genesis Chapter 5

From Adam to Noah

Fill-in-the-Blanks

This is the ***written*** account of Adam's line. When God created man, he made him in the likeness of God. He created them male and female and blessed them. And when they were ***created***, he called them man. When Adam had lived 130 years, he had a son in his own ***image***; and he named him Seth. After Seth was born, Adam lived 800 years and had other sons and daughters. Altogether, Adam lived 930 years, and then he ***died***. When Seth had lived 105 years he became the father of Enosh. And after he became the father of Enosh, Seth lived ***807*** years and had other sons and daughters'. ***Altogether***, Seth lived 912 years and then he died. When Enosh had lived 90 years, he became the father of Kenan. And after he ***became*** the father of Kenan, Enosh lived 815 years, and then died. When Kenan had lived 70 years, he became the father of Mahalalel. And ***after*** he became the father of Mahalalel, Kenan lived 840 years and had other sons and daughters. Altogether, Kenan lived 910 years, and then he died. When ***Mahalalel*** had lived 65 years, he became the father of ***Jared***. And after he became the father of Jared, Mahalalel lived ***830*** years and had other sons and daughters. Altogether, ***Mahalalel*** lived 895 years, and then he died. When Jared had lived 162 years, he became the father of Enoch. And after he became the father of ***Enoch***, Jared lived 800 years and had ***other*** sons and daughters. Altogether, Jared lived ***962*** years, and then he died. When Enoch had lived 65 years, he became the father of Methuselah. And after he became the father of ***Methuselah***, Enoch walked with God 300 years and had other sons and daughters. Altogether, Enoch lived 365 years. Enoch ***walked*** with God; then he was no more because God took him ***away***. When Methuselah had lived 187 years, he became the father of ***Lamech***. And after he became the father of Lamech, Methuselah lived 782 years and had other sons and daughters. Altogether, Methuselah lived 969 ***years***, and then he died. When Lamech had lived 182 years, he had a son. He named him Noah and said, "He will comfort us in the labor and ***painful*** toil of our hands ***caused*** by the ground the Lord has cursed." After Noah was born, Lamech lived 595 years and had other sons and daughters. Altogether, Lamech lived ***777*** years, and then he died. After Noah was 500 years old, he became the father of ***Shem***, ***Ham*** and ***Japheth***.

Genesis Chapter 5

From Adam to Noah

1. This is the written account of Adam's line.

2. When God created man, he made him in the likeness of God. He created them male and female and blessed them. And when they were created, he called them man.

3. When Adam had lived 130 years, he had a son in his own image; and he named him Seth. After Seth was born, Adam lived 800 years and had other sons and daughters. Altogether, Adam lived 930 years, and then he died.

4. When Seth had lived 105 years he became the father of Enosh. And after he became the father of Enosh, Seth lived 807 years and had other sons and daughters. Altogether, Seth lived 912 years and then he died.

5. When Enosh had lived 90 years, he became the father of Kenan. And after he became the father of Kenan, Enosh lived 815 years, and then died.

6. When Kenan had lived 70 years, he became the father of Mahalalel. And after he became the father of Mahalalel, Kenan lived 840 years and had other sons and daughters. Altogether, Kenan lived 910 years, and then he died.

7. When Mahalalel had lived 65 years, he became the father of Jared. And after he became the father of Jared, Mahalalel lived 830 years and had other sons and daughters. Altogether, Mahalalel lived 895 years, and then he died.

8. When Jared had lived 162 years, he became the father of Enoch. And after he became the father of Enoch, Jared lived 800 years and had other sons and daughters. Altogether, Jared lived 962 years, and then he died.

9. When Enoch had lived 65 years, he became the father of Methuselah. And after he became the father of Methuselah, Enoch walked with God 300 years and had other sons and daughters. Altogether, Enoch lived 365 years. Enoch walked with God; then he was no more because God took him away.

10. When Methuselah had lived 187 years, he became the father of Lamech. And after he became the father of Lamech, Methuselah lived 782 years and had other sons and daughters. Altogether, Methuselah lived 969 years, and then he died.

11. When Lamech had lived 182 years, he had a son. He named him Noah and said, "He will comfort us in the labor and painful toil of our hands caused by the ground the Lord has cursed." After Noah was born, Lamech lived 595 years and had other sons and daughters. Altogether, Lamech lived 777 years, and then he died.

12. After Noah was 500 years old, he became the father of Shem, Ham and Japheth.

Genesis Chapter 6

The Flood

ABC ORDER	SPELLING DEFINITIONS
Corrupt	Immoral and perverse; depraved; dishonest and venal; rotting; putrid; containing mistakes or alterations, as a text; to ruin or undermine the honesty or integrity of; to make morally impure; pervert; to taint; contaminate; to cause to become rotten; spoil; to alter the original form of a text; to damage data in a file or on a disk; to become corrupt.
Covenant	A binding agreement made by two or more persons or parties; compact; a formal sealed contract or agreement; a suit to recover damages for violation of such a contract; to promise by a covenant; to enter into a covenant; contract.
Grieve	To cause to be sorrowful; distress; to mourn or sorrow for; to hurt; harm; to feel grief; mourn.
Mortal	Liable or subject to death; of or relating to humans; of, relating to, or associated with death; causing death; fatal; implacable; unrelenting; of great intensity or severity; dire; conceivable; used as an intensifier.
Nephilim	A race of giants.
Pitch	To throw, usu. in a specific direction; toss; to throw the ball from the mound to the batter; to play a game or part of one in the position of pitcher; to put up in position; establish; to set firmly; implant; to fix the level of; to set the character and course of; to set at a specified downward slant, as the angle of a roof; to set in a particular key; to lead a card, thus establishing the trump suit; to sell or present a high-pressure fashion; to throw away; discard; to throw or toss something, as a ball, horseshoe, or bale; to play in the position of pitcher; to take a plunge or fall, esp. forward; to lurch or stumble; to buck, as a horse; to dip bow and stern alternately; to revolve about a lateral axis so that the nose lifts or descends in relation to the tail; used of an airplane; to revolve about a lateral axis that is both perpendicular to the longitudinal axis and horizontal to the earth; used of a space vehicle; to slope downward; to set up living quarters; encamp; to make a casual, usu. hurried choice or decision; to set to work vigorously; to join forces with others; cooperate; to attack verbally or physically; assault; an act or instance of pitching; a throw the ball by the pitcher for action by the batter; a ball so thrown; the rectangular area between the wickets in cricket, 20 meters by 3 meters or 22 yards by 10 feet; the alternate dip and rise of a ship's bow and stern; a step downward slant; the degree of such a slant; the angle of a roof; the highest point of

	a structure; a level or degree of development or intensity; the subjective quality of a sound, dependent primarily on the frequency, and to a lesser extent on the intensity of position of a tone in a scale, as determined by its frequency; a standard that establishes a frequency for each tone, used in the tuning of instruments; the distance traveled by a machine screw in a single revolution; the distance between two corresponding propeller would travel in an ideal medium during one complete revolution, measured parallel to the shaft of the propeller; an often hard-sell talk, as by a salesperson; an advertisement; the stand of a vendor or hawker; the game of seven-up.
Righteous	Meeting the standards of what is right and just; morally right; genuine; true; righteous individuals as a group.
Store	A place where merchandise is offered for sale; shop; a supply reserved for future use; supplies, esp. of food, clothing, or arms; a place where commodities are kept; a great number or quantity; abundance; to reserve or put away for future use; to fill, supply, or stock; to deposit or receive in a storehouse or warehouse for safekeeping; to copy data into memory or onto a storage device; forthcoming; to regard with esteem; value.
Violence	Physical force employed so as to violate, damage, or abuse; an act or instance of violent behavior or action; intensity or severity, as in natural phenomena; abusive or unjust use of power; abuse or injury to meaning content, or intent; fervor; vehemence.
Wickedness	Having or resulting from bad moral character; evil; sinful; immoral; depraved; vicious. Generally bad, painful, etc. but without any moral considerations involved.

Unscrambled Words:
Store
Corrupt
Righteousness
Pitch
Violence
Covenant
Mortal
Wickedness
Nephilim
Grieve

Genesis Chapter 6

The Flood

1. When men began to increase on earth and daughters were born to them, the sons of God saw that the daughters of men were beautiful, and they married any of them they chose.

2. The Lord said, "My Spirit will not contend with man forever, for he is mortal; his days will be a hundred and twenty years."

3. The Nephilim were on the earth in those days and also afterward when the sons of God went to the daughters of men and had children by them.

4. They were the heroes of old, men of renown.

5. The Lord saw how great man's wickedness on the earth had become, and that every inclination of the thoughts of his heart was only evil all the time.

6. The Lord was grieved that he had made man on the earth and his heart was filled with pain.

7. The Lord said, "I will wipe mankind, whom I have created, from the face of the earth men and animals, and creatures that move along the ground, and birds of the air for I am grieved that I have made them." But Noah found favor in the eyes of the Lord.

8. This is the account of Noah: Noah was a righteous man, blameless among the people of his time, and he walked with God. Noah had three sons: Shem, Ham and Japheth.

9. The earth was corrupt in Gods sight and was full of violence. God saw how corrupt the earth had become, for all the people on earth had corrupted their way.

10. God said to Noah, "Because of this corruption: I am going to put an end to all people, for the earth is filled with violence because of them. I am surely going to destroy both them and the earth.

11. The Lord told Noah to make Yourself an ark of Cypress wood.

12. The Lord instructed Noah to make rooms in it and coat it with pitch inside and out.

13. The Lord instructed Noah this is how you are to build it: The ark is to be 450 feet long, 75 feet wide and 45 feet high. Make a roof for it and finish the ark to within 18 inches of the top. Put a door in the side of the ark and make lower, middle and upper decks.

14. The Lord instructed Noah to build this ark because He was going to bring floodwaters on the earth to destroy all life under the heavens, every creature that has the breath of life in it.

15. The Lord stated everything on earth will perish.

16. The Lord stated He would establish His covenant with Noah, and Noah will enter the ark he and his sons and his wife and his sons' wives with him.

17. The Lord instructed Noah to bring into the ark two of all living creatures, male and female, to keep them alive with him. Two of every kind of bird, of every kind of animal and every kind of creature that moves along the ground will come to him to be kept alive.

18. The Lord instructed Noah to take every kind of food that is to be eaten and store it away as food for him and for them."

19. Yes, Noah did everything just as God commanded him.

Genesis Chapter 7

The Flood (cont.)

ABC ORDER	SPELLING DEFINITIONS
Ark	The chest containing the Ten Commandments written on stone tablets, carried by the Hebrews during their desert wanderings; the Holy Ark; the boat God commanded Noah to build for shelter during the flood; a large, commodious boat; a shelter or refuge.
Enter	To come or go into; to penetrate; pierce; to introduce; insert; to become a part of or an element in; to embark on; begin; to obtain admission to; to gain admission for; to enroll; to register as an entry in a competition or exhibition; to become a participant in; to take part as a contestant in; to make a beginning in; to place formally upon the records; to go upon in order to take possession of land; to reentry; to become a member of a group; to participate; to be a part or component of; to consider; investigate; to become party to contract; to set out; embark; to go upon in order to take legal possession of land; to begin to deal with or consider a subject.
Escape	To break free from confinement; to issue from confinement; leak out; to avoid a serious or unwanted outcome; to grow beyond a cultivated area; to interrupt a command, exit a program or change levels within a program by pressing the escape key; to get free of; to succeed in avoiding; to elude the memory or comprehension of; to issue involuntarily from; an act or instance of escaping, a worry, care, or unpleasantness; a gradual effusion from an enclosure; leakage; a cultivated plant established away from cultivation; a key on a keyboard pressed to interrupt a command, exit a program, or change levels within a program.
Female	Of, relating to, denoting the sex that produces ova or bears young; typical of or appropriate to the female sex; feminine; consisting of members of the females sex; relating to or designating an organ, as a pistil or ovary, that functions in producing seed or spores after fertilization; bearing pistils but not stamens; indicating or having a part, as a receptacle, designed to receive a complementary male part, as a plug; a member of the sex that produces ova or bears young; a woman or girl; a plant having only pistillate flowers.

Flood	An overflowing of water onto normally dry land; flood tide; an abundant flow or outpouring; floodlight; in the Bible, the covering of the earth with water that occurred during the time of Noah; to cover or submerge with or as if with a flood; inundate; to fill with an abundance or an excess; to become inundated or submerged; to pour forth.
Generation	The act or process of generating, esp. procreation, origination, or production; offspring sharing a common parent or parents and forming a single stage of descent; a group of contemporaneous individuals; a group of individuals considered as sharing a common contemporaneous cultural or social attribute; the average time interval between the birth of parents and the birth of the offspring; the technique of generating programs; the formation of a line or geometric figure by the movement of a point or line.
Male	Of, relating to, or designating the sex that has organs to produce spermatozoa for fertilizing ova; of or typical of the male sex; masculine; manly; virile; made up of men or boys or both; relating to or designating organs, as stamens or anthers, that are capable of fertilizing female organs; bearing stamens but not pistils; staminate; designed to be inserted into a recessed part or socket, as an electric plug; an individual of the sex that begets young by fertilizing ova; a man or boy; a plant bearing only staminate flowers.
Mate	One of a matched pair; a spouse; one of a conjugal pair of animals or birds; one of a pair of good friends or close companion; a person with whom one shares living quarters; a deck officer on a merchant ship ranking below the master; a US Navy petty officer who is an assistant to warrant officer; to join closely; pair; to unite in marriage; to pair animals for breeding; to become joined in marriage; to become mated.
Nostrils	Either of the external openings of the nose, through which air is inhaled and exhaled.
Pairs	Two corresponding persons or items, similar in form or function and matched or associated; one object consisting of two joined, similar parts that are dependent on each other; two persons who are married, engaged, or dating; two persons having something in common and considered together; two mated animals; two animals joined together in work; two playing cards of the same denomination; two members of a deliberative body with opposing opinions on a given issue who offset each other by agreeing to abstain from voting on the issue; an electron pair; to arrange in sets of two; couple to join in a pair; mate; to provide a partner for; to form a pair or pairs; to join as mates in marriage.

Unscrambled Words:
Nostrils
Pairs
Enter
Escape
Ark
Mate
Generation
Flood
Male
Female

Genesis Chapter 7

The Flood (cont.)

1. The Lord then said to Noah, "Go into the ark, you and your whole family because I have found you righteous in this generation. Take with you seven of every kind of clean animal, a male and its mate, and two of every kind of unclean animal, a male and its mate, and also seven of every kind of bird, male and female, to keep their various kinds alive throughout the earth. Seven days from now I will send rain on the earth for forty days and forty nights, and I will wipe from the face of the earth every living creature I have made."

2. Yes, Noah did all that the Lord had commanded him to do.

3. Noah was six hundred years old when the floodwaters came on the earth.

4. Noah and his sons and his wife and his son's wives entered the ark to escape the waters of the flood.

5. Pairs of clean and unclean animals, of birds and of all creatures that move along the ground, male and female, came to Noah and entered the ark, as God had commanded Noah.

6. After seven days the floodwaters came on the earth.

7. In the six hundredth year of Noah's life, on the seventeenth day of the second month—on that day the springs of the great deep burst forth, and the floodgates of the heavens were opened. And rain fell on the earth forty days and forty nights.

8. On that very day Noah and his sons, Shem, Ham, and Japheth, together with his wife and the wives of his three sons, entered the ark; they had with them every wild animal according to its kind, everything with wings. Pairs of creatures that have the breath of life in them

came to Noah and entered the ark. The animals going in were male and female of every living thing, as God had commanded Noah.

9. The Lord shut the door.

10. For forty days the flood kept coming on the earth, and as the waters increased they lifted the ark high above the earth.

11. The waters rose greatly on the earth, and all the high mountains under the entire heavens were covered. The waters rose and covered the mountains to a depth of more than twenty feet.

12. Every living thing that moved on the earth perished; birds, livestock, wild animals, all the creatures that swarm over the earth, and all mankind.

13. Everything on dry land that had the breath of life in it; nostrils died.

14. Every living thing on the face of the earth was wiped out; men animals and the creatures that move along the ground and the birds of the air were wiped from the earth.

15. Only Noah was left and those with him in the ark.

Genesis Chapter 8

The Flood (cont.)

ABC ORDER	SPELLING DEFINITIONS
Aroma	The fragrance of plants, or other substances; a pleasant, often spicy odor; a distinctive, usu. pleasant odor; a distinctive, intangible quality; aura.
Cease	To put an end to; discontinue; to come to an end; stop.
Curse	An appeal for evil or injury to befall someone or something; evil or injury resulting from or as if from an invocation; one that is accursed; something bringing or causing evil; scourge; a profane oath; an ecclesiastical censure, ban, or anathema; menstruation; to invoke evil, calamity, or injury upon; damn; to swear at; to bring evil upon; afflict; to put under an ecclesiastical ban or anathema; excommunicate; to utter curses; swear; that deserves to be cursed; wicked.
Endure	To carry on through despite hardships; undergo; to bear with tolerance; to continue in existence; last; to suffer patiently without yielding; lasting durable; unresolved; chronic; long-suffering.

Harvest	The act or process of gathering a crop; the crop that ripens or is gathered in a season; the amount or measure of the crop gathered in one season; the time or season of such gathering; the consequence or result of an action; to gather a crop; to gather a crop from; to take or kill fish as for food or population control; to extract from a culture or body, esp. for transplantation; to receive the consequences of an action; to gather a crop.
Inclination	An attitude or disposition toward something; a trend or general tendency toward a particular aspect, condition, or character; something for which one has a preference or leaning; the act of inclining, as a bow; the state of being inclined; tilt; a deviation from a horizontal or vertical direction; the degree of deviation from a horizontal or vertical.
Recede	To move back or away from a limit, point, or mark; to slope backward; to become or seem to become farther away; to withdraw or retreat; to yield or grant to one previously in possession; cede back.
Seedtime	A time for sowing seeds; a time of new growth or development.
Surface	The exterior face of an object; a material layer constituting such an exterior face; the boundary of a three-dimensional figure; the two-dimensional locus of points located in three-dimensional space; a portion of space having length and breadth but no thickness; superficial or outward appearance; relating to or occurring on or near the surface of the earth; merely apparent or opposed to real; superficial; to form the surface of, as by smoothing or leveling; to provide with a surface; to rise to the surface; to emerge after concealment.
Visible	Capable of being seen; obvious to the eye; apparent; manifest; on hand; available; made or intended to keep important parts in easily accessible view; represented visually, as by symbols.

Unscrambled Words:
Cease
Surface
Curse
Seedtime
Inclination
Aroma
Endure
Recede
Visible
Harvest

Genesis Chapter 8

The Flood (cont.)

1. God remembered Noah and all the wild animals and the livestock that were with him in the ark, and he sent a wind over the earth, and the waters receded.

2. The springs of the deep and the floodgates of the heavens had been closed, and the rain had stopped falling from the sky.

3. The water receded steadily from the earth. At the end of the hundred and fifty days the water had gone down, and on the seventeenth day of the seventh month the ark came to rest on the mountains of Ararat.

4. The waters continued to recede until the tenth month, and the first day of the tenth month, the tops of the mountains became visible.

5. After forty days Noah opened the window he had made in the ark and sent out a raven, and it kept flying back and forth until the water had dried up from the earth.

6. Then Noah sent out a dove to see if the water had receded from the surface of the ground. But the dove could find no place to set its feet because there was water over all the surface of the earth; so it returned to Noah in the ark.

7. Noah reached out his hand and took the dove and brought it back to himself in the ark.

8. Noah waited seven more days and again sent out the dove from the ark, when the dove returned to him in the evening, there in its beak was a freshly plucked olive leaf. Then Noah knew that the water had receded from the earth.

9. Noah waited seven more days and sent the dove out again, but this time it did not return to him.

10. By the first day of the first month of Noah's six hundred and first years, the water had dried up from the earth.

11. Noah then removed the covering from the ark and saw that the surface of the ground was dry.

12. By the twenty-seventh day of the second month the earth was completely dry.

13. God said to Noah, "Come out of the ark, you and your wife and your sons and their wives; bring out every kind of living creature that is with you; the birds, the animals, and all the creatures that move along the ground; so they can multiply on the earth and be fruitful and increase in number upon it."

14. So Noah came out, together with his sons and his wife and his sons wives.

15. All the animals and all the creatures that move along the ground and all the birds everything that moves on the earth came out of the ark, one kind after another.

16. Then Noah built an altar to the Lord and, taking some of all the clean animals and clean birds, he sacrificed burnt offerings on it.

17. The Lord smelled the pleasing aroma and said in his heart: "Never again will I curse the ground because of man, even though every inclination of his heart is evil from childhood. And never again will I destroy all living creatures, as I have done."

18. The Lord states as long as the earth endures the following eight things will never cease:

    a. Seedtime.
    b. Harvest time.
    c. Cold.
    d. Heat.
    e. Summer.
    f. Winter.
    g. Night.
    h. Daytime.

Genesis Chapter 9

The Sons of Noah

ABC ORDER	SPELLING DEFINITIONS
Beast	An animal; a large four-footed animal; animal nature; a brutal person.
Between	In the interval or position separating; intermediate to, as in quantity, amount, or degree; connecting spatially; in confidence restricted to; by the combined effect or effort; in the combined ownership of; as measured against; used often to express a reciprocal relationship; in an intermediate space, position, or time; in the interim; in an intermediate situation.
Bloodshed	The shedding or spilling of blood; slaughter; the injury or killing of humans.
Earth	The land surface of the world; the softer, friable part of land; soil; the third planet from the sun, having a sidereal period of revolution about the sun of 365.26 days at a mean distance of 92.96 million miles or approx. 149 million kilometers, an axial rotation period of 23 hours 56.07 minutes, an equatorial radius of 3,963 miles or approx . . . 6,378 kilometers, and a mass of 5.974 x 10.24 kilograms; the dwelling place of mortals; the human inhabitants of the world; worldly pursuits and affairs; the material body of a human as opposed to the spirit; the den of a burrowing animal; the ground of an electrical circuit; a metallic oxide, as alumina or zirconia, that is difficult to reduce and was once held to be an element; to cover plants with soil for protection; to chase into an underground hiding place; to hide or burrow in the ground, as a hunted animal; realistic; sensible; to hunt and run down.

Establish	To make secure or firm; to set in a secure condition or position; to cause to be recognized and accepted; to found; to make a state institution of a church; to introduce and enforce a law; to prove the truth of.
Extend	To open or straighten out; unbend; to stretch or spread out to full length; to exert oneself completely; to cause to move at full gallop; to increase in bulk or quantity by adding a cheaper substance; to adulterate; to expand the area or scope of; to increase the influence of; to make more comprehensive or inclusive; to make available; provide; to prolong the time of repayment; to assess or evaluate; appraise; to seize or make a levy on for the purpose of settling a debt; to stretch or reach; stretch or spread out; continued; for a long period of time; protracted; extensive in meaning, scope or influence.
Fruitful	Producing fruit; producing abundantly; conducive to productivity; producing results; profitable.
Rainbow	An arc of spectral colors appearing in the sky opposite the sun as a result of the refractive dispersion of sunlight in raindrops or mist; a similar arc, as in a waterfall mist or graded display of colors; an illusory hope; an arc resembling a rainbow formed by moonlight.
Slave	One bound in servitude to a person or household as an instrument of labor; one who is submissive or subject to a person or influence; an extremely hard worker; a machine or component controlled by another machine or component; to work like a slave.
Territory	An area of land; region; the land and waters under the jurisdiction of a government; a part of the United States that is not admitted as a state, that is administered by a governor and that has its own legislature; a semi-automatic geographic region, as a colonial possession, that is dependent on an external government; an area for which one is responsible as representative or agent; the area of a field defended by a sports team; an area inhabited by an individual animal or a mating pair or group of animals, and often vigorously defended against intruders; a sphere of interest; province.

Unscrambled Words
Extend
Territory
Slave
Between
Bloodshed
Beast
Rainbow
Fruitful
Earth
Everlasting

Genesis Chapter 9

Gods covenant with Noah/The Sons of Noah

Gods covenant with Noah

1. God blessed Noah and his sons, saying to them, "Be fruitful and increase in number and fill the earth. The fear and dread of you will fall upon all the beasts of the earth and all the birds of the air, upon every creature that moves along the ground, and upon all the fish of the sea; they are given into your hands. Everything that lives and moves will be food for you. Just as I gave you the green plants, I now give you everything."

2. God stated to Noah concerning what he must not eat: "You must not eat meat that has its lifeblood still in it."

3. God states to Noah concerning lifeblood, "For your life blood I will surely demand an account. I will demand an account from every animal. And for each man, too, I will demand an account for the life of his fellow man."

4. God states to Noah concerning shedding blood in the land: "Whoever sheds the blood of man, by man shall his blood be shed; for in the image of God has God made man."

5. God states as for Noah, "be fruitful and increase in number; multiply on the earth and increase upon it."

6. Then God said to Noah and his sons with him: "I now establish my covenant with you and with your descendants after you and with every living creature that was with you the birds, the livestock and all the wild animals, all those that came out of the ark with you; every living creature on earth."

7. God states he establish this covenant with Noah: "Never again will all life be cut off by the waters of a flood to destroy the earth."

8. God said to Noah concerning the sign of the covenant: "This is the sign of the covenant I am making between Me and you and every living creature with you, a covenant for all generations to come; I have set My rainbow in the clouds, and it will be the sign of the covenant between Me and the earth. Whenever I bring clouds over the earth and the rainbow appears in the clouds, I will remember My covenant between Me and you and all living creatures of every kind. Never again will the waters become a flood to destroy all life. Whenever the rainbow appears in the clouds, I will see it and remember the everlasting covenant between God and all living creatures of every kind on the earth."

9. So God said to Noah, "This is the sign of the covenant I have established between Me and all life on the earth."

The Sons of Noah

10. The sons of Noah who came out of the ark were:

   a.   Shem.
   b.   Ham.
   c.   Japheth.

11. Ham was the father of Canaan.

12. These were the three sons of Noah, and from them came the people who were scattered over the earth.

13. Noah, a man of the soil, proceeded to plant a vineyard and when he drank some of its wine, he became drunk and lay uncovered inside his tent.

14. Ham, the father of Canaan, saw his father's nakedness and told his two brothers outside.

15. Shem and Japheth took a garment and laid it across their shoulders; then they walked backward and covered their father's nakedness. Their faces were turned the other way so that they would not see their father's nakedness.

16. When Noah awoke from his wine and found out what his youngest son had done to him, he said, "Cursed be Canaan! The lowest of slaves will he be to his brothers." He also said: "Blessed be the Lord, the God of Shem! May Canaan be the slave of Shem. May God extend the territory of Japheth; may Japheth live in the tents of Shem and may Canaan be his slave."

17. After the flood Noah lived 350 years; altogether, Noah lived 950 years, and then he died.

Genesis Chapter 10

Answer Key

ABC ORDER	SPELLING DEFINITIONS
Canaanite	In the bible, any person descended from Canaan, the son of Ham; a member of a Semitic people who inhabited the ancient region of Canaan from late prehistoric times and were conquered by the Israelites around 1000BC; the Semitic language of the Canaanites.
Clan	A traditional social unit in the Scottish Highlands made up of a number of families claiming a common ancestor and following the same hereditary chieftain; a division of a tribe tracing descent from a common ancestor; a large group of relatives, friends, or associates.

Descent	The act or an instance of descending; a way down; a downward incline or passage; slope; hereditary derivation; lineage; the fact or process of coming down or being derived from a source; development in form or structure during transmission from an original source; one generation of a specific lineage; transference of property by inheritance; a lowering or decline, as in status or level; a sudden attack; onslaught.
Hamites	A person regarded as descended from Ham; a member of a group of related peoples inhabiting northern and northeastern Africa, including the Berbers and the descendants of ancient Egyptians.
Japhethites	Any of Japheth's descendants.
Region	A large, usu. continuous portion of a surface or space; area; a large, indefinite area of the earth's surface; a particular district or territory; a field of interest or activity; sphere; a part of the earth marked by distinctive animal or plant life; an area of the body with natural or arbitrarily assigned boundaries.
Semites	Of, belonging to, or characteristics of the Semites; a member of any of the peoples whose language is Semitic, including the Hebrews, Arabs, Assyrians, Phoenicians, Babylonians, etc.
Stretched	To widen, lengthen, or distend by pulling to cause to extend from one place to another or across a given space; to make taut; tighten; to extend or reach forth; to extend oneself or one's extremities at full length; to flex the muscles of; to exert to the utmost; strain; to wrench or strain a muscle; to put to torture on the rack; to extend or broaden quantity of by admixture or dilution; to extend or reach over a distance or plain; to lie down at full length; to flex or extend one's limbs or muscles; to extend over a given period of time; the act of stretching or the state of being stretched; the extent to which something can be stretched; elasticity a continuous or unbroken length, area, or expanse; a straight section off a racecourse or track, esp. the section leading to the finish line; a continuous time period; a prison term; the last stage of an event, period, or process; the movement in which a pitcher raises both hands to the height of the head and then lowers them to the waist for a short pause before pitching the ball, used esp. when runners are on base.
Territory	An area of land; region; the land and waters under the jurisdiction of a government; a part of the United States that is not admitted as a state, that is administered by a governor and that has its own legislature; a semi-automatic geographic region, as a colonial possession, that is dependent on an external government; an area for which one is responsible as representative or agent; the area of a field defended by a sports team; an area inhabited by an individual animal or a mating pair or group of animals, and often vigorously defended against intruders; a sphere of interest; province.
Warrior	A man experienced or engaged in warfare; a fighting man; one who is engaged aggressively or energetically in an activity, cause, or conflict.

Unscrambled Words:
Territory
Region
Stretched
Descent
Warrior
Japhethites
Semites
Clan
Hamites
Canaanites

Genesis Chapter 10

Answer Key

1. The name of Japheth's descendants were the Japhethites

2. The name of Ham descendants were the Hamites

3. The name of Shem's descendants were the Semites

4. The name of Canaan's descendants were the Canaanites

5. Japheth's seven sons were:

   a. Gomer
   b. Magog
   c. Madai
   d. Javan

   e. Tubal
   f. Meshech
   g. Tiras

6. The names of Gomer's sons were:

   a. Askenaz
   b. Riphath

   c. Togarmah

7. The names of Javan sons were:

   a. Elishah
   b. Tarshish

   c. The Kittim
   d. The Rodanim

8. These were people that allowed maritime people to spread into their territories. So they lived among the maritime people.

9. Ham's four sons names were:

   a. Cush
   b. Mizraim

   c. Put
   d. Canaan

10. Cush six sons names were:

    a. Seba
    b. Havilah
    c. Sabtah
    d. Raamah
    e. Sabteca
    f. Nimrod

11. The names of Raamah's sons were:

    a. Sheba   b. Dedan

12. Nimrod was the son of Cush who grew into a mighty warrior.

13. He was a mighty hunter warrior before the Lord.

14. The first center of Nimrod's kingdom was Babylon.

15. The sons of Shem were:

    a. Elam
    b. Asshur
    c. Arphaxad
    d. Lud
    e. Aram

16. The four sons of Aram were:

    a. Uz
    b. Hul
    c. Gether
    d. Meshech

17. The names of Eber's two sons were:

    a. Peleg   b. Joktan

18. Peleg was given this name because in this time the earth was divided.

19. Joktan's thirteen sons were named:

    a. Almodad
    b. Sheleph
    c. Hazarmaveth
    d. Jerah
    e. Hadoram
    f. Uzal
    g. Diklah
    h. Obal
    i. Abimael
    j. Sheba
    k. Ophir
    l. Havilah
    m. Joba

20. They dwelled in the region of Mesha toward Sephar, in the eastern hill country.

21. Later the Canaanites clan scattered and the borders of Canaan reached from Sidon toward Gerar as far as Gaza and then towards Sodom, Gomorrah, Admah and Zeboiim, and as far as Lasha.

22. The name of Arphaxed's son was:

    a. Shelah

23. The name of Shelah's son was:

    a. Eber

24. Nimrod built the city of Nineveh in Assyria.

25. The seven nations Mizraim became the father of are:

    a. The Ludite   d. The Naphtuhites   g. The Caphtorites

    b. The Anamites   e. The Pathrusites

    c. The Lehabites   f. The Casluhites

26. The name of Canaan's firstborn was:

    a. Sidon

27. The eleven nations Canaan became the father of are:

    a. Sidon his first born   e. The Girgashites   i. The Arvadites

    b. The Hittites   f. The Hivites   j. The Zemarites

    c. The Jebusites   g. The Arkites   k. The Hamathites

    d. The Amorites   h. The Semites

Genesis Chapter 1-10 Review

Who am I?

1. I am Jesus   5. I am Seth   8. I am Eve

2. I am Lemech   6. I am Cain   9. I am the serpent

3. I am Adam   7. We are Shem and Japheth   10. I am Able

4. I am Noah   11. I am Hem

<u>*Genesis Chapter 1-10 Review*</u>

<u>*Part I: Written Essay-Optional/Opinionated.*</u>

<u>*Part II. Biblical Background*</u>

Give a brief synopsis of all that was done by God on each day as written in chapters 1 & 2 of the Zondervan Study Bible:

The Seven Days of Creation	
Day 1:	{Genesis 1:3-5} And God said, "Let there be light," and there was light. God saw that the light was good, and He separated the light from the darkness. God called the light "day" and the darkness He called "night". And there was evening, and there was morning—the first day.
Day 2:	{Genesis 1:6-8} And God said, "Let there be an expanse between the waters to separate water from water." So God made the expanse and separated the water under the expanse from the water above it. And it was so. God called the expanse "sky," and there was evening and there was morning the second day.
Day 3:	{Genesis 1:9-13} And God said, "Let the water under the sky be gathered to one place, and let dry ground appear." And it was so. God called the dry ground "land," and the gathered waters He called "seas," and God saw that it was good. Then God said, "Let the land produce vegetation; seed-bearing plants and trees on the land that bear fruit with seed in it, according to their various kinds. And it was so. The land produced vegetation: plants bearing seed according to their kinds. And God saw that is was good. And there was evening and there was morning—the third day.
Day 4:	{Genesis 1:14-19} And God said, "Let there be lights in the expanse of the sky to separate the day from the night, and let them serve as signs to mark seasons and days and years, and let them be lights in the expanse of the sky to give light on the earth." And it was so. God made two great lights—the greater light to govern the night. He also made the stars. God set them in the expanse of the sky to give light on the earth, to govern the day and the night, and to separate light from darkness. And God saw that it was good. And there was evening, and there was morning—the fourth day.

Day 5:	{Genesis 1:20-23} And God said, "Let the water teem with living creatures, and let birds fly above the earth across the expanse of the sky." So God created the great creatures of the sea and every living and moving thing with which the waters teems, according to their kinds, and every winged bird according to its kind. And God saw that it was good. God blessed them and said, "Be fruitful and increase in number and fill the water in the seas, and let the birds increase on the earth. And there was evening, and there was morning the fifth day.
Day 6:	{Genesis 1:24-31} And God said, "Let the land produce living creatures according to their kinds: livestock, creatures that move along the ground, and wild animals, each according to its kind." And it was so. God made the wild animals according to their kinds, the livestock according to their kinds, and all the creatures that move along the ground according to their kinds. And saw that it was good. Then God said let us make man in our image, in our likeness and let them rule over the air, over the livestock, over all that move along the ground." So God created man in his own image, in the image of God He created him; male and female He created them. God blessed them and said to them, "Be fruitful and increase in number; fill the earth and subdue it. Rule over the fish of the sea and the birds of the air and over every living creature that moves on the ground." Then God said, "I give you every seed-bearing plant on the face to the whole earth and all birds of the air and all the creatures that move on the ground—everything that has breath of life in it—I give every green plant for food." And it was so. God saw all that He had made, and it was very good. And there was evening and there was morning—the sixth day.
Day 7:	{Genesis 2:2-3} By the seventh day God had finished the work he had been doing; so on the seventh day he rested from all his work. And God blessed the seventh day and made it holy, because on it He rested from all the work of creating that He had done.

Part III. Historical Research

Using your Zondervan Study Bible list some of the well-known people and events of the Old Testament from Genesis chapters 1-10 then write a brief synopsis of why they are known and accurately recorded in the Bible:

Well Known people in the Bible—Genesis 1-10	
Well known person	*Brief synopsis*
Optional/Opinionated	*Optional/Opinionated*
Optional/Opinionated	*Optional/Opinionated*
Optional/Opinionated	*Optional/Opinionated*

Optional/Opinionated	Optional/Opinionated
Optional/Opinionated	Optional/Opinionated

Well Known Events in the Bible—Genesis 1-10

Well known events:	Brief synopsis
Optional/Opinionated	Essay Optional/Opinionated
Optional/Opinionated	Essay Optional/Opinionated
Optional/Opinionated	Essay Optional/Opinionated
Optional/Opinionated	Essay Optional/Opinionated
Optional/Opinionated	Essay Optional/Opinionated
Optional/Opinionated	Essay Optional/Opinionated
Optional/Opinionated	Essay Optional/Opinionated

Part IV. Biblical Remembrance

1. Genesis
2. Exodus
3. Leviticus
4. Numbers
5. Deuteronomy
6. Joshua
7. Judges
8. Ruth
9. 1st Samuel
10. 2nd Samuel
11. 1st Kings
12. 2nd Kings
13. 1st Chronicles

14. 2nd Chronicles
15. Ezra
16. Nehemiah
17. Esther
18. Job
19. Psalms
20. Proverbs
21. Ecclesiastes
22. Song of Songs
23. Isaiah
24. Jeremiah
25. Lamentations
26. Ezekiel

27. Daniel
28. Hosea
29. Joel
30. Amos
31. Obadiah
32. Jonah
33. Micah
34. Nahum
35. Habakkuk
36. Zephaniah
37. Haggai
38. Zechariah
39. Malachi

There are five books of Pentateuch/Law:

6. Genesis
7. Exodus
8. Leviticus
9. Numbers
10. Deuteronomy

> The first five books of the Bible are the books of Law recorded to inform all about the beginning of creation, God's commandments, covenants, promises, blessings, and deliverance for those of righteousness, as well as, God's destruction for man's disobedience. As Adam's disobedience brought about death to all who follow the wiles of the devil, Noah's belief and obedience brought about covenants to all generations; Abraham's faith brought about blessings and promises to all nations, which lead to the coming of our Lord and Savior Jesus Christ whose obedience to be a sacrificial atonement for the sins of all the nations brought Salvation, Redemption, Freedom, and the dispensation of Mercy and Grace.

There are twelve books of History:

13. Joshua
14. Judges
15. Ruth
16. 1ˢᵗ Samuel
17. 2ⁿᵈ Samuel
18. 1ˢᵗ Kings
19. 2ⁿᵈ Kings
20. 1ˢᵗ Chronicles
21. 2ⁿᵈ Chronicles
22. Ezra
23. Nehemiah
24. Esther

> *The next twelve books are the books of history recorded to give encouragement and assurance of God's rewards for the obedience of the people; to illustrate the importance and value of godliness, obedience, loyalty, and faithfulness among the nations; warnings of destruction as well as, the consequences for disobeying God and His commandments; and to illustrate that God is a God of restoration and deliverance to all who obey His commandments and walk in obedience, godliness, loyalty, and faithfulness unto Him; as well as, a God of destruction to all who turn from Him and disobey His commands and ordinances.*

There are twelve books of Prophecy. The first five books of prophecy are the books of Major Prophets:

6. Isaiah
7. Jeremiah
8. Lamentations
9. Ezekiel
10. Daniel

> *The next five books are the books of prophecy recorded to warn Israel of the judgments that were to come, have come, and is still to come, visions of the prophets, illustrates the loss of Israel's land, city, and temple because of disobedience, the importance of repentance and hope. These prophetic revelations have been prophetically revealed to the apostle John in the book of Revelation to warn all of what is to come. These books reveal the coming of our Messiah in Isaiah 9:6 "This child born unto us has brought Salvation, Redemption, and Freedom of sins through repentance for all nations who follow the commands/Laws of God."*

The next twelve books of prophecy are the books of the Minor Prophets:

13. Hosea
14. Joel
15. Amos
16. Obadiah
17. Jonah
18. Micah
19. Nahum
20. Habakkuk
21. Zephaniah
22. Haggai
23. Zechariah
24. Malachi

> *The next twelve books are the books of the minor prophets recorded to warn all of the adulteries of Judah and Israel; call all to repentance of sins; help us to understand that God loves all, to give hope to all; to bring forth self-examination as God examines the hearts and mind of mankind; to help us to understand the value of God's mercy. As written in Jonah 4:2 God gives warning before destruction that you may repent and be saved.*

There are five books of Poetry:

6. Job
7. Psalms
8. Proverbs
9. Ecclesiastes
10. Song of Songs
Or Song of Solomon

> *The next five books are the books of poetry/wisdom recorded to illustrate the sovereignty of God's faithfulness even in times of our trials and tribulations. These books of poetry/wisdom help us to understand God's guidance, blessings, and provision for all who endure to the end. These books include the God-given wisdom, hymns, proverbs, and worship of Israel while demonstrating the importance of prayer, praise, and worship unto God as it is our prayer, praise, and worship unto God which activates the manifestation of our blessings through communication with our Lord and Savior.*

* Note the books of Psalm are not categorized as chapter and verses like all the other books of the Bible. The Books of Psalms are classified as five books and one hundred-fifty divisions:

Book 1: Divisions 1-41
Book 2: Divisions 42-72
Book 3: Divisions 73-89
Book 4: Divisions 90-106
Book 5: Divisions 107-150